The Insurance Information Institute's HANDBOOK for REPORTERS

LYNN BRENNER

Printed in the United States of America.
Revised second printing, 1995.

Library of Congress Cataloging-in-Publication Data

Brenner, Lynn.
The Insurance Information Institute's handbook for reporters/
Lynn Brenner.
p. cm.
ISBN 0-932387-38-1 : $22.50
1. Insurance – United States – Handbooks, manuals, etc. I. Title.
HG8531.B733 1993
368'.973–dc20 93-5909
CIP

The Handbook for Reporters is published by the Insurance Information Institute, a primary source for information, analysis and referral on insurance subjects. Western Insurance Information Service (WIIS), which is affiliated with the Insurance Information Institute, provides consumer information services in 10 western states.

Foreword

Each year the staff of the Insurance Information Institute handles over 4,000 information requests from journalists representing some 1,700 media outlets, in addition to about 50,000 requests from other interested parties and the general public. I.I.I. is recognized by the media, governments, regulatory organizations, universities and the public as a basic source of factual information, analysis and referral on insurance subjects.

The central function of the Institute is to provide insurance information that is accurate and timely. To that end we recently decided that in addition to responding to requests for information, it would be useful to provide a basic reference work on insurance-related topics that journalists frequently ask about — topics such as earthquakes and hurricanes, industry trends and financial issues.

We asked Lynn Brenner to write the book because she is a respected journalist who has covered insurance for numerous publications and is known for the clarity and thoughtfulness of her writing as well as her wide knowledge of insurance. We are grateful to her and to our colleagues at many insurance organizations, companies and brokerage firms who worked with her, supplying perspective, information and encouragement. Particularly we wish to thank Rob Bier of the American Council of Life Insurance and Stephen Young of the Health Insurance Association of America, who reviewed sections of the book.

This book is intended to be used along with the latest edition of another Insurance Information Institute publication — *Insurance Facts*, the almanac of the property/casualty insurance industry. The "Fact Book," as *Insurance Facts* is commonly known, contains the latest available statistics related to the topics discussed in *The Handbook for Reporters*. Media representatives may obtain a free copy of the current Fact Book by dialing our special press number — 1-800-331-9146 — which is available for media questions 24 hours a day.

We hope this handbook together with the Fact Book proves useful and look forward to continuing to provide timely and accurate insurance information.

Gordon C. Stewart
President
Insurance Information Institute

Introduction

Insurance, once an obscure business beat, has become front page news. And it seems insurance will be even bigger news throughout the 1990s.

At least three insurance markets integral to the fabric of American life — automobile, workers compensation, and health insurance — are likely to undergo significant restructuring in the decade ahead.

In all three, underlying costs have outstripped inflation for more than a decade, making the coverage expensive to millions of Americans, and at the same time either only marginally profitable or unprofitable for some insurance companies.

To a large extent, these growing costs reflect fundamental changes in our society, including dramatic increases in litigation and crime, the development of expensive new medical technologies, the practice of defensive medicine, and shifting concepts of insurance as a right versus insurance as a business. The now widely-held view that coverages like health insurance are basic necessities to which all Americans are entitled also holds profound implications for insurance.

In broad terms, reporting on insurance in the coming decade will focus on how insurers, insurance regulators, consumer advocates, and state and federal lawmakers struggle to adapt traditional systems to sweeping social, political and economic changes.

To make it easy to use, this handbook is organized and cross-referenced by topic.

Under Auto insurance are found formal explanations of auto insurance rates, premiums, and losses; what an auto insurance policy covers; how an insurance buyer can qualify for premium discounts; statistics on auto theft; and cross-references to other entries that address auto insurance availability in urban areas, the profitability of auto insurance as a line of business, and various proposals to reform the auto insurance system, listed under Assigned risk plans, Investment income, Underwriting income, Proposition 103, No-fault, and Pay-at-the-Pump.

Under AIDS are the cost of treating AIDS and HIV-positive patients and information on how the disease is treated for life and health insurance purposes. For additional insurance information pertinent to stories about AIDS, cross-references lead to Accelerated death benefits and to Self-insurance/legal issues.

Under Property/casualty insurance are definitions of the two basic coverages and an explanation of the factors that affect profitability in both.

A section at the back gives the names and telephone numbers of insurance and non-insurance sources, including rating agencies and consumer groups, which can expand on and update all the information in the book.

Accelerated death benefits: *A life insurance policy option* also known as living benefits, *under which policy proceeds are paid to the insured person during his or her lifetime, instead of to a named beneficiary after his or her death.* By mid-1992, more than 150 life insurers offered this policy option, which is designed to respond to the needs of people coping with the enormous medical costs of terminal illnesses.

An accelerated death benefits option allows payment of some or all of the policy proceeds if the policyholder becomes terminally ill or incapacitated; needs extraordinary medical intervention, such as an organ transplant; or is confined to a nursing home. The accelerated benefits payment is deducted from the death benefit that is ultimately paid to the policyholder's beneficiary.

Life insurance proceeds paid after a policyholder's death are exempt from federal income tax. In March 1993, the Internal Revenue Service proposed regulations that would give the same tax-exemption to life insurance policy living benefits paid to policyholders with terminal illnesses, and the regulation is expected to be formalized before the end of 1993. (See **AIDS**)

Accident and health insurance: *Coverage for accidental injury, accidental death, and health expenses.* Policy benefits may include payment for preventive services, hospital and medical expenses, catastrophic care and income payments, up to specified limits.

Accounting: Insurers use two kinds. *Generally accepted accounting principles (GAAP) accounting is used in financial statements that publicly-held companies prepare for the Securities and Exchange*

Commission. But *state laws require that statutory accounting methods be used in financial statements for insurance regulators.* These laws are designed to protect policyholders by imposing a high solvency standard — statutory accounting is more conservative than GAAP accounting. For example, statutory accounting requires that selling expenses be recorded immediately, rather than amortized over the life of the policy, to track with premiums as they are earned.

Actual cash value: *Insurance under which the policyholder receives an amount equal to the replacement value of damaged property minus an allowance for depreciation.* Unless a homeowners policy specifies that property is covered for its replacement value, the coverage is for actual cash value.

Actuary: *An insurance professional who specializes in statistical information.* Actuaries are responsible for determining rates and rating methods and for evaluating insurance company reserves.

Adjuster: *A person employed by a property / casualty insurer to evaluate losses and settle policyholder claims.* Not to be confused with a public adjuster, who is an independent businessperson who negotiates claims settlements with insurers on behalf of policyholders, and receives a portion of the claim settlement in return.

Administrative Services Only (ASO): Corporations that self-insure pay their losses from their own assets. But they frequently buy *insurance services that are ancillary to risk assumption, such as claims administration and loss control engineering.* Insurers say that such a client is buying Administrative Services Only. For insurers, ASO business is neither as potentially profitable nor as risky as underwriting financial loss. It's a source of fee income, generating predictable cash flow. (See **Captives; Self-insurance**)

Admitted company: *An insurance company licensed and authorized to do business in a particular state.*

Adverse Selection: *The tendency of those who are risk prone to obtain or continue coverage more than those who are less likely to have a claim.* An obvious example is earthquake insurance — homeowners on an earthquake fault line are the likeliest buyers of the policy. Insurers avoid adverse selection, which drives up losses (and premiums) because it concentrates risk instead of spreading it.

Sometimes when a risk involves adverse selection, government steps in to assure that coverage will be provided. The federal government provides flood coverage, for example. (See **Catastrophe/floods**)

Agency companies: See **Agent, Insurance company**

Agent: Insurance is sold by two types of agents. *Independent agents are self-employed business people who typically represent two or more insurance companies and are paid on a commission basis.* An agency company is a company that markets products via independent agents.

Exclusive agents represent only one insurance company. They may be salaried employees or work on a commission basis. Companies using exclusive agents are called direct writers. (See **Broker**)

The market share of direct writers has grown for more than a decade. In 1991, they represented 43 percent of the property/casualty market, and agency companies accounted for 57 percent of the market.

AIDS: The medical treatment of Americans who have AIDS or are HIV-positive cost $10.3 billion in 1992, according to the U.S.

Agency for Health Care Policy and Research. By 1995, this cost is expected to reach $15.2 billion.

The life and health insurance industries have taken the position that AIDS should be treated no differently for insurance purposes than any other illness. Currently, both life and health insurers can legally deny coverage to an applicant who has any fatal disease.

But in health insurance, this probably won't be the case much longer. A primary goal of the Clinton Administration is health care reform that guarantees universal access to coverage for all Americans, regardless of their state of health. Universal access would eliminate denial of coverage based on preexisting medical conditions, and is strongly supported by the health insurance industry.

Currently, insurance applicants who are HIV-positive or have AIDS, like others with catastrophic illnesses, cannot buy health coverage in the regular market. But they can buy it from Blue Cross/Blue Shield Associations during their periods of open enrollment, when all applicants are guaranteed coverage, and from high-risk health insurance pools for people unable to buy coverage in the regular market. High-risk pools exist in about half the states. Before the Clinton Administration took office, the Health Insurance Association of America was working to develop them throughout the country. (See **Accelerated death benefits; Self-Insurance/legal issues; Case management**)

Airplane insurance: Commercial airlines carry *a combination of property insurance on airplanes and liability insurance for negligent acts and / or omissions by the airline that result in bodily injury or property damage to passengers, and to individuals who are not passengers.* Damage to the airplane is covered both on the ground and in the air, as long as it is caused by a risk that is not specifically excluded in the policy. Exclusions include wear and tear; piloting the aircraft by someone not described in the policy; operating it outside stipulated geographical boundaries; and damage and destruction resulting from war, riots, strikes, civil commotions, mechanical breakdown, and structural failure.

Alien insurance company: *An insurance company incorporated under the laws of a foreign country.* (A "foreign" insurance company is one domiciled, i.e., incorporated in another state.)

Allied lines: *Property insurance that is usually bought in conjunction with a fire insurance policy.* Allied lines include wind, water damage, and vandalism coverages.

Alternative markets: See **Self-insurance**

Annuity: *A life insurance company contract that pays a periodic income benefit — annual, semiannual, quarterly or monthly — either for a specific period of time or for the annuitant's lifetime.* Annuity investments grow tax-deferred. No taxes are due until income payments begin. Annuities are often used to accumulate retirement savings. Some also allow tax-free loans against the accumulated contract value.

From a life insurer's viewpoint, an annuity presents the opposite mortality risk from life insurance. Life insurance pays a benefit when the policyholder dies. An annuity is designed to pay for as long as the annuitant lives. With both products, the insurer's profit or loss depends on making accurate assumptions about the buyer's life expectancy and the insurance company's investment returns and expenses.

Annuity contracts offer a wide variety of premium and benefit payment schedules and investment options. An annuity can be bought for a single payment or a series of periodic payments. Benefits can be scheduled to begin immediately after purchase, or deferred to begin at a specific future date, such as when the annuitant turns 65. Benefits can last for the lifetime of one or two individuals or for a specified period of time.

Fixed-income annuities are invested in the insurer's general investment account. Many variable annuities let the buyer select his or her own investments from a menu of bond, stock and mutual funds. These mutual funds are legally segregated accounts, owned by their shareholders. They are legally protected should the insurer become insolvent. (See **Life insurance; Structured settlement**)

Antitrust laws: *Laws that prohibit companies from working as a group to set prices, restrict supplies, or otherwise engage in activities that would restrict competition in the marketplace.* The insurance industry is subject to state antitrust laws, but has a limited exemption from federal antitrust law. This exemption, contained in the McCarran-Ferguson Act, permits insurers to jointly develop common insurance forms and share loss data to help them price their own individual policies. (See **Statistical data**)

Far from being dominated by a few firms, the insurance business is highly competitive. At the beginning of this decade, there were some 3,900 companies selling property and casualty insurance, and no single company or group had more than a 15 percent share of the market. The 10 largest companies accounted for less than 45 percent of the market. There are more than 2,000 life insurers, and some 1,500 health insurers in the United States. The 10 biggest life insurance companies account for some 40 percent of life insurance in force.

The insurance industry is not unique in having a limited exemption to federal antitrust law. Other industries and groups that have similar exemptions include labor, agriculture, sports, and to a certain extent, banking. (See **McCarran-Ferguson; Regulation**)

Apportionment: *The dividing of a loss proportionately among two or more insurers which cover the same loss.*

Appraisal: *A survey to determine a property's insurable value, or the amount of a loss.*

Arbitration: *A procedure in which an insurance company and an insured agree to settle a dispute over a claim settlement* by accepting as binding a decision made by a disinterested person who is selected by two appraisers — each of whom is appointed by one of the parties to the dispute.

Arson: *The deliberate setting of a fire,* arson causes in excess of $1 billion a year in property losses. It is the known cause of 25.7 percent of fires in non-residential structures, including schools and restaurants, and the largest known cause of non-residential fire deaths.

Law enforcement sources estimate that only 14 percent of all arson suspects are motivated by a desire to collect insurance. Typical arsonists are very young; nearly half of those arrested for arson are under age 18, and 64 percent are under 25. According to the Federal Bureau of Investigation, only about 15 percent of arson cases are ever closed, either by an arrest or a predominance of the evidence.

The nation's biggest property/casualty companies are members of the Insurance Committee for Arson Control, an organization that acts as a catalyst for the industry's anti-arson efforts, and as a liaison to other groups devoted to arson control.

Assets: *The property owned by an insurance company,* including stocks, bonds and real estate investments. State laws don't allow insurers to list all their assets on their balance sheets in stating the book value of what they own. Assets that can't be included (called "non-admitted assets") include furniture, fixtures, agents' debt balances and accounts receivable that are more than 90 days past due.

Assigned risk plans: All 50 states and the District of Columbia have *facilities in which drivers can obtain auto insurance, if they are unable to buy it in the regular or "voluntary" market.* Every insurer licensed in the state must participate in these facilities, which are variously known as assigned risk plans or joint underwriting facilities, and often referred to as the residual market. When residual market premiums are too low to cover its losses, insurers are usually assessed to make up the difference. These additional costs are passed on to all their customers. (Source: Automobile Insurance Plans Service Office)

Residual markets also exist for other types of coverage, including property insurance in locations where the risk of riot, theft, vandalism, arson, or severe storm damage is substantial. (See **Fair Plans; Beach and Windstorm Plans**)

Assumption reinsurance: *A transaction, sometimes called a policy transfer, in which one life insurance company sells a block of policies, annuities or other products, to another.*

Auto insurance: *Protection for the owner of a car.* Auto physical damage insurance is coverage for damage to or loss of a car, because of collision, fire, theft, and other perils. Auto liability insurance is coverage for financial loss due to liability for injuries to others or damage to their property, caused by the policyholder's car.

Auto insurance accounts for more than $4 out of every $10 of total premiums for property/casualty insurance. For more than a decade, auto premiums have risen sharply, making coverage expensive to millions of drivers. But losses have climbed even faster than premiums. As a result, auto insurance is only marginally profitable for many of the companies that sell it.

There's a growing consensus that substantive changes are needed in the auto insurance system, but little agreement about what they should entail. Proposed reforms include state-mandated rate rollbacks (see **Proposition 103**), more stringent laws limiting auto insurance litigation (see **No-fault**) and a national system in which drivers would pay for insurance through a gasoline tax. (See **Pay-at-the-Pump**)

Auto insurance premium discounts: The surest way for a driver to save money on auto insurance is to shop around. Premiums vary widely from one company to another. Many insurance companies also give premium discounts to drivers who:

—have a good driving record
—have taken driver education courses
—are between the ages of 50 and 74
—car pool
—insure several cars on one policy
—buy homeowners or renters insurance from the same company
—install anti-theft devices in their cars
—drive cars with safety features like automatic seat belts and air bags (See **Auto safety**)

Auto insurance profitability: For many insurers, auto coverage hasn't been profitable in recent years. (See **Underwriting income; Investment income**) According to a study by the National Association of Insurance Commissioners, insurers' return on net worth for private passenger auto insurance averaged 8.3 percent between 1985 and the end of 1991.

Auto losses: The cost of auto insurance claims has roughly doubled every decade. This rate of increase reflects galloping inflation in both medical and auto repair bills, as well as sharp increases in the frequency of auto theft, and a steadily rising number of liability claims. Between 1980 and 1988, for example, the cost of settling claims, including defense costs, more than doubled — from $3.2 billion in 1980 to $7.5 billion in 1988. (Sources for updated numbers: I.I.I., A.M. Best, Insurance Services Office, Conning & Co.)

Auto policy: It can (but doesn't have to) include coverage for up to six distinct risks, each of which is priced separately. They are:

1. Bodily injury liability, for injuries the policyholder causes to someone else.
2. Medical, or in some states, Personal Injury Protection (PIP) for treatment of injuries to the driver and passengers of the policyholder's car. At its broadest, PIP can cover medical payments, lost wages, and the cost of replacing services normally performed by someone injured in an auto accident.
3. Property damage liability, for damage the policyholder caused to someone else's property.
4. Collision, for damage to the policyholder's car from a collision.
5. Comprehensive, for damage to the policyholder's car that doesn't involve a collision with another car. Covered risks include fire, theft, falling objects, missiles, explosion, earthquake, flood, riot and civil commotion.
6. Uninsured motorists coverage, for treatment of the policyholder's injuries as a result of collision with an uninsured driver.

No state requires car owners to carry insurance for all these risks. But many states require drivers to carry minimum amounts of liability insurance for bodily injury and property damage, as well as personal injury protection coverage. (See **Financial responsibility law; No-fault**)

Auto premiums: Insurers base their auto premiums — *the price charged for coverage* — on historical loss experience for similar risks. The idea is to charge the highest prices to classes of policyholders who can be expected to have the highest insured losses.

The characteristics that demonstrably affect the frequency and the cost of losses are: the driver's age, sex, marital status and driving record; where he or she lives; the make and model of the car; and whether the car is used for commuting, business, pleasure or farming. All these factors are used to make up a driver's insurance rate. The ultimate premium charged adds factors for inflation, and for the insurer's administrative and sales expenses and profit.

Private passenger auto premiums vary enormously, not only from insurer to insurer, but also from one driver to another. Many drivers pay much higher than average premiums, for reasons sometimes beyond their control, such as their age and where they live — factors that substantially increase the frequency and severity of claims. (See **Rate**) In densely populated urban areas, where auto theft is six and a half times more common than in the nation's smallest cities, accidents are more frequent, and auto repair and medical care more expensive, auto insurance has become very expensive for many drivers. (See **Assigned risk plans; Proposition 103**)

Both insurance industry and government studies show that on average, auto premiums haven't kept pace with losses. Between 1980 and 1988, for example, losses per insured car grew 94.9 percent, while the average premium increased 79 percent. (See **Investment income**)

Auto safety: A motor vehicle death occurs on average once every 12 minutes and an injury every 20 seconds, according to the National Safety Council. Motor vehicle accidents are the fourth leading cause of death for all ages throughout the nation. They account for more than 40 percent of deaths in the 16 to 22 age group. Drivers over age 74 are also at greater risk of causing fatal accidents. Older drivers drive fewer miles than younger ones. But Department of Transportation statistics show that based on the miles they drive, older drivers have a higher rate of fatal accidents.

That's likely to become a matter of increasing public concern and debate in the next 10 years: In 1990, 22 million licensed drivers were over 65. During this decade, the number of drivers over 65 will increase.

In 1992, the Insurance Institute for Highway Safety opened a world-class Vehicle Research Center near Charlottesville, Virginia. The Center's purpose is to find ways to save lives and prevent injuries and property damage in crashes.

Auto safety legislation: The insurance industry is a leading supporter of federal and state efforts to improve all aspects of automobile and highway safety. Consistent use of seat belts and strict enforcement of drunk driving laws would prevent thousands of deaths, reduce the severity of hundreds of thousands of injuries, and save insurance companies and insurance buyers millions of dollars every year.

(Sources: For comprehensive statistical information on the number and cost of auto accidents, and their causes, call the National Safety Council and the Insurance Institute for Highway Safety. For information on the relative safety of different makes and models of cars, and the cost of repairing them, call the Highway Loss Data Institute (HLDI). HLDI data show that the safest cars are big four-door models, station wagons, passenger vans, and cars equipped with air bags and other passive restraint systems.)

Auto theft: A car is stolen somewhere in the United States every 19 seconds. Like everyone else, thieves have preferences among cars, and those preferences are carefully tracked by the Insurance Institute for Highway Safety. One among many examples:

There were more than seven times as many theft claims for the 1990 four-door Volkswagen Jetta as for all other 1990 models combined. But these claims, although frequent, were relatively small; stolen radios accounted for many of them. Owners of big Fords, Mercuries, and Lincolns, on the other hand, filed fewer but much more expensive theft claims than Jetta owners. Thieves didn't prey on the Fords, Mercuries and Lincolns as often. But when they did, they didn't limit themselves to radios — they stole the cars. Sources: For a list of last year's most frequently stolen cars, call the Highway Loss Data Institute. The National Insurance Crime Bureau is also a good source for information related to vehicle theft.

Balance sheet: An insurance company's balance sheet shows its financial condition at a specific point in time. The balance sheet *lists the company's assets* — such as its investments and its reinsurance, *and its liabilities*, such as loss reserves to pay claims in the future. The balance sheet also states the company's equity known as policyholder surplus. Changes in surplus are considered a basic indicator of an insurer's financial health. (See **Capital & surplus**)

Beach and Windstorm Plans: Like FAIR Plans, which provide basic property insurance coverage, these are state-sponsored *insurance pools that sell property coverage for the peril of windstorm to people unable to buy it in the voluntary market because of their high exposure to risk.* Seven states along the Atlantic and Gulf Coasts have Beach and Windstorm Plans that cover residential and commercial properties against hurricanes and other windstorms. In all these states insurance company participation in the plans is mandatory.

The value of insured property in hurricane-risk areas is now so great that, depending on where it strikes, one hurricane could be as financially devastating to the property/casualty industry as a major California earthquake. In 1992, for example, Hurricane Andrew caused $15.5 billion in insured losses — the industry's biggest single catastrophic loss up to that time. But if Hurricane Andrew had struck 20 miles farther north than it did, the total insured loss could easily have been three times as great.

An industry-sponsored group called the Natural Disaster Coalition has urged the adoption of a federal reinsurance program. Under the Natural Disaster Coalition's proposal, insurers would pay premiums in exchange for federal reinsurance to assume catastrophic losses after a specified threshold was reached. (Source: Property Insurance Plans Service Office) (See **Catastrophe/earthquakes; Reinsurance**)

Blanket coverage: *Insurance coverage for more than one item of property at a single location, or two or more items of property in different locations.*

Boiler and machinery insurance: See **Commercial lines**

Broker: *An intermediary between a customer and an insurance company who represents the insurance buyer.* The broker typically searches the market for coverage appropriate to his or her client. Like insurance agents (who represent the insurance company), brokers work on commission. Unlike agents, brokers typically sell commercial rather than personal insurance. Some life insurance policies are sold by securities brokers, who must also be licensed to sell insurance. (See **Agent**)

Burglary and theft insurance: *Insurance for loss of property due to burglary, robbery, or larceny.* This type of insurance is one of many coverages provided in the standard homeowners policy and in the special multiperil policy, which covers businesses.

Business insurance: See **Commercial lines**

Business interruption insurance: See **Commercial lines**

C

Capacity: Insurance industry capacity is *the supply of insurance available to meet demand.* Capacity depends on the industry's financial ability to accept risks. When there's little capacity, insurance premiums are high and the insurance buyers face a hard market. High premiums help increase insurer profitability, which eventually attracts new capacity to the market. New capacity means more competition among insurers, which brings premiums down, eventually leading to a soft market. The ensuing underwriting losses eventually drive capacity from the market and the entire cycle is repeated. (See **Property/casualty cycle; Reinsurance**)

Capital & surplus: In a publicly-held insurance company, capital is shareholders' equity. In a mutual company, which is owned by its policyholders, capital is retained earnings. In both cases, policyholders' surplus is what's left when the insurer's other liabilities — unearned premiums and reserves for unpaid claims — are subtracted from its assets — earned premiums, reinsurance, and investments. Surplus is the financial cushion that protects a company's policyholders in case of unexpectedly high claims.

Historically, a three-to-one premium-to-surplus ratio — $3 of written premium for each $1 of surplus — has been considered a benchmark of surplus adequacy for property/casualty insurance. There is no single equivalent measure of capital adequacy in life insurance. (See **Solvency; Early warning system**)

Each state has its own minimum capital and surplus requirements. Insurance regulators are reluctant to let insurers with inadequate surplus take on new business. But reasonable people can disagree about the adequacy of an insurer's surplus, because a key determinant of surplus is the insurer's reserves for losses — a number that can only be estimated. Under-reserving for losses inflates company surplus. Over-reserving for losses makes surplus appear smaller than it really is. (See **Risk-based capital**)

Captives: *Insurers that are created and wholly-owned by one or more non-insurers, for the primary purpose of providing their owners with coverage.* By the end of the 1980s, captives and other forms of self-insurance accounted for about one-third of U.S. insurance premiums. Providing administrative services to captives has become an important source of fee income for many insurance brokers and insurance companies. (See **Self-insurance**)

Case management: *A system of coordinating and supervising the medical services used to treat a patient in order to improve the quality of care and reduce its cost.* The case manager coordinates health care delivery and financing for the patient, acting as his or her advocate with medical providers, and as an adviser to members of the patient's family involved in his or her care. (See **Health insurance/managed care**)

Cash value life insurance: See **Life insurance products**

Casualty insurance: See **Property/casualty insurance**

Catastrophe: To insurers, a catastrophe is *a single incident, or series of related incidents, causing insured property losses totaling more than $5 million.* Insurance actuaries calculate the probability of catastrophic loss on a state-by-state basis, using a formula based on the total number of catastrophes in each state over a 40-year period. This catastrophe factor, calculated annually, is included in the price of insurance. Before Hurricane Andrew, for example, Florida homeowners insurance had a 14 percent catastrophe factor, accounting for $50 out of the average premium of $344.

The insurance industry is able to absorb the multibillion dollar losses caused by hurricanes, earthquakes, and other natural disasters, because those losses are spread among thousands of companies thanks to worldwide catastrophe reinsurance. Insurers' ability and willingness to sell coverage fluctuates with the availability and cost of the catastrophe reinsurance they buy. After Hurricane Andrew, for example, the availability of catastrophe reinsurance became extremely limited.

The federal government sometimes acts as an ultimate reinsurer when the capacity of the private insurance and reinsurance markets is insufficient to cover a risk. Past examples of federal reinsurance have included riot and crime coverages in urban areas, and liability coverage for nuclear power plants. Currently, the federal government is the reinsurer for flood and crop-hail coverages. The insurance industry strongly supports legislative proposals to extend federal reinsurance to earthquake and windstorm coverages.

The stock prices of publicly-held insurance companies frequently rise after a major hurricane or earthquake takes place during a prolonged soft market, i.e., a buyer's market for insurance coverage. The reason: Wall Street anticipates that insurers will raise their rates as a result of the losses, setting the stage for future profitability. (See **Reinsurance; Catastrophe/earthquakes**)

Catastrophe policies: Much of the damage caused by natural disasters is covered by ordinary homeowners multiperil policies and commercial multiperil policies. (See **Homeowners multiperil insurance; Commercial lines**) But some is not. Separate coverage must be purchased for damage caused by floods and earthquakes. Windstorm is covered in standard policies, but consumers and businesses with property in highly vulnerable areas will pay more for the coverage, because their catastrophe factor will be higher. (See **Catastrophe**)

Many homeowners and businesses don't carry earthquake and flood coverage. When reporting dollar losses in the wake of these natural disasters, it's important to distinguish between total losses and total insured losses. (See **Beach and Windstorm Plans; Catastrophe/earthquakes, floods, hailstorms, hurricanes, tornadoes, volcanic eruptions**)

Catastrophe/earthquakes: The United States experiences only two percent of the world's earthquakes, but some 90 percent of its population lives in seismically active areas. Since 1900, earthquakes have occurred in 39 states and they have caused damage in all 50.

Predicting earthquakes is not an exact science. In late 1992, geophysicist Steven Ward of the University of Southern California rated the risk of an earthquake registering 7.5 on the Richter Scale in the southern part of the San Andreas fault at 19 percent over the next 30 years.

A report released earlier by a research group included a representative of the U.S. Geological Survey, which analyzes and predicts earthquakes for the Federal Emergency Management Agency (FEMA), said there's a 47 percent chance that an earthquake registering 7.0 will hit the Southern San Andreas Fault within a five year period.

The potential insured loss is enormous. One reason is that the insured values in this area are so great. Another is that an earthquake of that magnitude would trigger simultaneous losses in so many different lines of coverage. A major earthquake would cause multiple fires, injuries in the workplace, and automobile crashes on highways. Claims would be triggered under auto, fire, business interruption, workers compensation, as well as life and health insurance policies. The effect on the nation's insurers — and on their customers — could be devastating.

The Natural Disaster Coalition, an industry-sponsored organization, strongly supports Congressional proposals to create a federal earthquake reinsurance program that would be funded by insurers, and pay for earthquake losses that exceed a predetermined amount.

Catastrophe/earthquake policies: Earthquake insurance is available even in highly vulnerable areas, but it is expensive. It carries a 10 percent deductible that applies separately to a building and its contents. In other words, a policy covering a house for $50,000 and its contents for $25,000 requires the policyholder to pay for the first $5,000 of damage to the house and the first $2,500 of damage to the contents.

Catastrophe/floods: Floods cause enormous financial losses, but often they're not insured. One reason: People who own property in areas that are not prone to flooding often mistakenly assume flood damage is covered in standard homeowners policies. Homeowners policies cover damage from windstorms, including wind-driven rain, but insurance against flooding damage must be bought separately.

People who do own flood insurance but haven't actually read the policies sometimes assume coverage is broader than it is. Flood insurance policies are catastrophe coverage, and provide much more limited coverage than standard homeowners policies. Flood insurance doesn't automatically cover the contents of a building, for example. Contents coverage against flood damage must be bought for an additional premium.

Homeowners and commercial multiperil policies purchased by business owners typically cover water damage, but not when it results from a flood. This distinction resulted in conflicting interpretations of policy language after the April 1992 freak flood in downtown Chicago forced most of the business district to shut down.

A contractor for the city of Chicago installing pilings in the Chicago River inadvertently ruptured an underwater tunnel, part of a network of turn-of-the-century tunnels underneath downtown Chicago. The rupture caused massive flooding throughout the tunnel network, the sub-basements of downtown buildings and extensive parts of the subway system. Because the flood in question wasn't the result of natural causes, most, but not all, insurers decided the water damage it caused was covered. An estimated $300 million was paid for insured property and business interruption losses.

Flood insurance coverage is provided by the federal government. It's sold under the National Flood Insurance Program, and is available to both homeowners and businesses. Private insurance companies sell Federal Insurance Administration (FIA) flood policies for a commission, but don't pay the claims. To qualify for flood insurance, property must be located in a community that participates in the federal flood control program. (Sources: Federal Insurance Administration, Federal Emergency Management Agency).

Catastrophe/hailstorms: Homeowners and auto insurance policies both cover damages caused by hailstorm, a major risk in the Mountain States and the Midwest. The most expensive hailstorm to date hit Denver in July 1990, accompanied by tornadoes. The total insured damage was $625 million, mainly due to automobile losses.

Catastrophe/hurricanes: A hurricane is a windstorm with 75 or more mile-per-hour winds — and windstorm is covered in standard homeowners policies. But consumers who live in areas particularly vulnerable to hurricane damage may have to buy separate coverage. (See **Beach and Windstorm Plans**)

In only two years of this century — 1927 and 1962 — has the Gulf of Mexico been free of a hurricane. The two costliest insured hurricanes to date were Hugo, which hit South Carolina in August 1989, and Andrew, which hit Florida in September 1992. Hurricane Hugo ultimately cost $4.2 billion in insured losses. Hurricane Andrew cost $15.5 billion.

Catastrophe/nuclear accidents: Business, homeowners and auto insurance policies exclude damage caused by nuclear contamination. But consumers are covered for this risk through insurance carried by the operators of nuclear power plants and other commercial nuclear facilities throughout the United States.

This coverage is provided by two special insurance pools. American Nuclear Insurers (ANI) and Mutual Atomic Energy Liability Underwriters (MAELU). The two pools were formed in 1957, in response to the Price-Anderson Act, which required operators of nuclear reactors to demonstrate financial ability to respond to liability for property damage or bodily injury to the public caused by nuclear material used in connection with their facilities.

Under this Act, the federal government originally provided up to $500 million of coverage above the limits available from the insurance industry. This federal coverage was eventually phased out after the capacity to cover the risk reached $560 million. In 1975, a second layer of mandatory protection from private sources was introduced. This was comprised of assessments against all the U.S. utilities operating nuclear reactors, if the consequences of a nuclear accident at any such reactor exceeded the level of primary financial protection afforded by the pools. But the federal government's role as an ultimate source of coverage is unchanged. The 1975 amendment to the Price-Anderson Act also states that when damages exceed the limits of insurance coverage, "The Congress will . . . take whatever action is deemed necessary and appropriate to protect the public from the consequences at a disaster of such magnitude."

On August 20, 1988, President Reagan signed legislation renewing Price-Anderson for 15 years. The law increased each reactor operator's liability for assessments in a second layer of financial protection from $5 million to $66.15 million for each nuclear accident. The total amount of financial protection now exceeds $7.8 billion. The first $200 million of that total is provided by the nuclear insurance pools.

Since 1957, liability claim payments and loss adjustment expenses have totaled about $89.5 million, of which about $58.8 million represents payments resulting from the 1979 Three Mile Island incident.

Catastrophe/riot and civil commotion: Damages resulting from riot and civil commotion are covered under comprehensive auto, homeowners multiperil and commercial multiperil policies. The costliest property/casualty claims resulting from riot and civil commotion to date were for $775 million for insured losses caused by the civil disorder in Los Angeles from April 29 to May 4, 1992, after announcement of the verdict acquitting police in the Rodney King beating trial.

Standard property/casualty policies also cover damages caused by acts of terrorism, such as the 1993 bombing of the World Trade Center. But damages caused by acts of war are excluded from most policies. (See **War risk**)

Catastrophe/tornadoes: Tornadoes are windstorms with speeds up to 300 miles per hour. The tornado season runs from April to July, but tornadoes can strike at any time and anywhere. The nation's most devastating tornado killed 689 people in three states — Missouri, Illinois and Indiana — on March 18, 1925. Windstorm is covered in standard homeowners policies. (See **Beach and Windstorm Plans**)

Catastrophe/volcanic eruptions: Until the May 18, 1980 eruption of Mount St. Helens in Washington, volcanic eruption was excluded in some homeowners policies and not mentioned in others. Nevertheless, most property damage claims resulting from the Mount St. Helens eruption were paid. Since 1980, volcanic eruption has been added to standard policies as a covered peril.

Chartered Property/Casualty Underwriter: See **CPCU**

ChFC: *Chartered Financial Consultant, a professional designation conferred by The American College*, on financial services professionals who complete 10 fundamental courses in financial planning.

Claims, filing: Taking the right steps after an insured loss can speed up the process of settling a claim, especially after a natural disaster like an earthquake or hurricane. It's a good idea to:

1. Call your agent or insurance company representative and let him or her know where you can be reached. Inventory the losses as soon as possible. Make notes and take photos of damage.
2. Make temporary repairs to protect your belongings from further damage. Keep receipts.
3. Get the damage surveyed by your agent or company representative. Collect anything that might help document the original cost of damaged items — receipts, canceled checks, warranties. Provide the insurer with copies of documentation and contractors' estimates of repairs.
4. Don't get permanent repairs made until the adjuster has approved the price.
5. Hire licensed contractors to provide repair estimates and do the work.

On news stories about major events in which claimants are individual consumers and small businesses, as in the case of Hurricanes Andrew and Hugo, independent agents and small brokerage firms are a good source of information. When the claimants are corporations, as in the case of the 1991 Chicago flood and the 1993 bombing of New York City's World Trade Center, the big brokerage firms that specialize in commercial insurance are good sources of information.

Claims-made policy: *A form of an insurance policy that pays claims presented to the insurer during the term of the policy or within a specific time after its expiration.* By contrast, an occurrence policy pays claims arising out of incidents that occur during the policy term, even if the claims are filed many years later.

Casualty insurers introduced claims-made policies in the late 1970s to limit their exposure to unknown future liabilities. Many casualty claims aren't filed until years after a policy is written. An error in medical procedure, for example, may not be detected until long after the procedure is carried out. (See **Property/casualty insurance/profitability; Incurred But Not Reported losses; Pollution insurance**)

CLU: Chartered Life Underwriter, *a professional designation conferred by The American College.* Recipients must pass examinations in business courses, including insurance, investments and taxation, and must have professional experience in life insurance planning.

COBRA: See **Consolidated Omnibus Budget Reconciliation Act**

Coinsurance: 1. *In property insurance,* a coinsurance clause *requires the policyholder to carry insurance equal to a specified percentage of the value of the property in order to receive full payment on a loss.* 2. *In health insurance, coinsurance is a percentage of each claim, above the deductible, that is paid by the policyholder.* A 20 percent coinsurance clause in a health policy means that after the policyholder has paid the deductible, he or she will pay for 20 percent of the covered losses. The insurer will pay for 80 percent of covered losses, up to a specific dollar ceiling. After that ceiling is reached, the insurer pays 100 percent of covered losses, up to the policy limit.

Collateral source rule: See **Tort law**

Collision insurance: An optional auto insurance coverage which pays for damage to the policyholder's car caused by collision. (See **Auto insurance**) Collision insurance never pays for more than the market value of the car, so it makes sense for a new car, but not for an older one whose market value has deteriorated.

Combined ratio: The combined ratio is *the percentage of each premium dollar a property /casualty insurer spends on claims and expenses.* An example: In 1990, auto insurers' combined ratio for liability coverages was 118 percent. This means that $1.18 went in claims and expenses for every $1 of premium earned. When the combined ratio is over 100, the insurer has an underwriting loss. (See **Loss ratio; Expense ratio; Investment income; Underwriting income**)

Commercial General Liability Insurance (CGL): *A broad commercial policy covering all the liability exposures of a business that are not specifically excluded.* (An excluded coverage, for example, is for automobiles and trucks, which are covered under commercial automobile policies.) Among the exposures covered by CGL policies:

— Product liability, for the manufacturer and/or distributor's exposure to lawsuits by persons who have sustained bodily injury or property damage through use of the product.

— Completed operations coverage would pay for bodily injury or property damage caused by a completed project — the installation of new plumbing in a customer's house, for example. Completed operations protects a business that sells service rather than products against liability claims arising out of work performed away from the business premises.

— Premises and operations, for bodily injury or property damage occurring on the insured's premises and/or as a result of the insured's business operations — a slip-and-fall in a supermarket, for example, or a restaurant customer whose fur coat was ruined by a plate of food dropped by a waiter.

— Elevator coverage, for bodily injury incurred in an elevator or on an escalator on the insured's premises.

— Independent contractors coverage, for bodily injury caused by the negligent acts or omissions of an independent contractor employed by the insured. (See **Commercial lines; Pollution insurance**)

Commercial lines: *Insurance products that are designed for and bought by businesses,* as opposed to personal lines products, which are sold to individuals.

The main commercial lines of coverage are:

—**Boiler and machinery insurance**: This coverage is often called Equipment Breakdown, or Systems Breakdown insurance. It's *insurance for damage caused by the malfunction or breakdown,* not just *of boilers,* but of a vast array of other equipment a business depends on, including *air conditioning, heating, electrical, telephone, and computer systems.* (See **Commercial multiperil insurance**)

—**Business interruption insurance**: *Coverage that reimburses a business owner for lost profits and continuing fixed expenses during the time that his or her business must stay closed as a result of a named peril.* This insurance reimbursed covered businesses forced to stay closed after such catastrophes as the February 26, 1993 bombing of New York City's World Trade Center, and the April 29, 1992 Los Angeles riot.

—**Commercial multiperil insurance**, *a package policy that includes property, boiler and machinery, crime and general liability coverages.*

—**Comprehensive General Liability insurance (CGL)**, which *covers all liability risks of a business, except for those specifically excluded.* Among the exposures covered are liability for products, completed operations, premises and operations, elevators and independent contractors. Among the exposures excluded from CGL coverage is liability for pollution damage. (See **Pollution insurance**)

—**Directors and officers liability insurance**, *which covers directors and officers of a company for negligent acts or omissions or misleading statements that result in successful libel suits against the company.* The coverage includes the cost of defending against such suits.

—**Professional liability insurance**, *which covers specialists, such as accountants, lawyers, doctors, dentists, pharmacists and insurance brokers and agents for negligence and/or errors and omissions that injure their clients.* (See **Malpractice insurance**)

—**Property insurance** against *losses caused by specified perils, including fire, windstorm, hail, explosion, riot, vandalism, malicious mischief, riot and civil commotion, and smoke.*

—**Workers compensation** (See **Workers Compensation; Captives; Self-insurance**)

Commission: *The fee paid to the insurance salesperson, as a percentage of the policy premium.* Commissions are an important factor in the ultimate cost of the policy to the buyer, and its profit margin for the insurer. Sales fees on life insurance policies typically include a first-year sales commission and smaller annual renewal commissions for each year the policy is maintained. Agents also receive commissions for selling auto and homeowners policies, and subsequent smaller commissions in each year the policyholder renews coverage. The percentage of premium used to calculate a commission varies widely, depending on the type of coverage, the insurer, and the marketing method used. (See **Expense ratio**)

Community rating laws: See **Health insurance/profitability**

Competitive state fund: A facility established by a state to sell workers compensation insurance in competition with private insurers.

Compulsory insurance: See **Financial responsibility law**

Consolidated Omnibus Budget Reconciliation Act (COBRA): *A federal law under which group health plans sponsored by employers with 20 or more employees must offer continuation of coverage to employees who leave their jobs, voluntarily or otherwise, and their dependents.* The employee must pay the entire premium up to 102 percent of the cost of coverage extended under COBRA. Depending on circumstances, which are detailed in the law, COBRA permits employees to extend their own coverage for up to 18 months, and that of their surviving dependents for up to 36 months.

Contingent liability: *The liability of individuals, corporations or partnerships, for accidents caused by persons (other than employees)* *for whose acts or omissions the individuals, corporations or partnerships are legally responsible.*

Cost of insurance: See **Property/casualty insurance; Life insurance; Capacity; Investment income; Underwriting income; Rate**

Coverage: Another word for *insurance,* i.e., how much coverage a person has is the amount of insurance he or she carries.

CPCU: Chartered property/casualty underwriter, *a professional designation given by the American Institute for Property and Liability Underwriters.* Among requirements for the designation are successful completion of national examinations in insurance, risk management, economics, finance, management, accounting and law, as well as three years of work experience.

Credit insurance: *Coverage that pays off an outstanding loan in the event of the policyholder's death and/or makes loan payments if the policyholder is disabled.* Credit insurance typically is offered as an option in connection with credit card and auto loans and mortgages. Credit insurance shouldn't be confused with private mortgage insurance (PMI), which most banks require mortgage borrowers to carry until the equity in their homes reaches 20 percent of the loan outstanding. PMI protects the mortgage lender against loss in the event the borrower defaults on his or her loan.

Credit rating: See **Rating agencies; Financial guarantee insurance**

Crop-hail insurance: *Protection against damage to growing crops as a result of hail or certain other named perils.* Federally subsidized Multi-Peril Crop Insurance (MPCI) covers farmers against hailstorm, damage by insects, excessive moisture and drought.

Declaration: *The part of a property or liability insurance policy that states the name and address of the policyholder, the property insured, its location and description, the policy period (i.e., how long the coverage will stay in force), the amount of insurance coverage, the applicable premiums, and supplemental information provided by the insured.* It is often referred to as the "dec page."

Deductible: *The amount of loss paid by the policyholder.* A deductible can be a specified dollar amount, a percentage of the claim amount, or *a specified amount of time* that must elapse after the loss before the insurance policy starts paying benefits. Insurers typically offer a choice of deductibles in each policy. The bigger the deductible, the lower the premium charged for the same amount of coverage. A policy with no deductible is called first-dollar coverage and, when available, is very expensive.

Direct premiums: *Property/casualty premiums collected by the insurer from policyholders, before reinsurance is ceded to, or accepted from, another company.* Insurers share some of their direct premiums, along with some of the risk they represent, with their reinsurers. (See **Reinsurance**)

Direct writers: *Insurance companies that sell directly to the public, via their own employees or by exclusive agents.* (See **Agent**)

Directors and officers liability: See **Commercial lines**

Disability insurance: *A type of health insurance that pays a monthly income to the policyholder when he or she is unable to work because of an illness or accident.* Disability policies typically begin making payments after a specified waiting period has elapsed, and pay not more than 80 percent of the policyholder's total income before he or she became disabled, up to a maximum dollar amount. The duration of benefits varies with the policy.

Dividends to policyholders: Many life insurance policies and some property/casualty policies pay annual dividends to their owners. Dividends are *a partial premium refund,* not a taxable distribution. They're not guaranteed. Policies that pay dividends are called participating policies.

Domestic insurance company: *State regulators refer to any company domiciled in their state as a domestic company,* and to companies domiciled in other states as foreign companies. (A company domiciled in a foreign country is referred to as an "alien" insurer.)

DRG (diagnosis related groups) reimbursement: *A health insurance reimbursement system that pays medical providers specific fees based on the medical diagnosis of the insured patient, irrespective of actual provider costs.* DRG would specify the fee payable for an appendectomy, for example. The DRG method of reimbursement was introduced in 1982 by Medicare as a way of controlling medical costs by standardizing fees. (See **Health insurance/managed care**)

Early warning system: In an effort to spot potential financial problems at insurance companies as early as possible, the National Association of Insurance Commissioners has created *a system of measuring insurers' financial stability*. The Insurance Regulatory Information System, commonly known as IRIS, or "the early warning system," uses financial ratios to measure insurers' financial strength. IRIS is a recommendation of the National Association of Insurance Commissioners. Its use is up to each individual state insurance department. (See **Solvency**)

Earned premium: Insurance premiums typically are payable in advance and have not been fully earned until the policy period expires. Earned premium is *the portion of premium that applies to the expired part of the policy period*. One month after the purchase of a $1,200 annual policy, for example, the insurer's earned premium is $100, or one twelfth of the premium, and the unearned premium is $1,100.

Earthquake coverage: See **Catastrophe/earthquakes**

Economic loss: The *total financial loss resulting from a death or disability of a wage earner, or from destruction of property*. This total would include loss of earnings, medical expenses, funeral expenses, the cost of restoring or replacing property, and legal expenses. It is distinguished from noneconomic loss, such as the pain caused by an injury.

Endorsement: *A written form attached to an insurance policy that alters the policy's coverage, terms or conditions.*

Environmental impairment liability: *A form of insurance designed to cover losses and liabilities arising from damage to property caused by pollution.* (See **Pollution insurance**)

Errors and omissions coverage: *A professional liability policy covering the policyholder for negligent acts and/or omissions that may harm his or her clients.* An insurance agent's errors and omissions policy, for example, would protect him or her from liability for a failure to remit a premium to an insurer that resulted in loss of coverage for a client.(See **Commercial lines/professional liability insurance**)

Excess & surplus lines: See **Surplus lines**

Expense ratio: *The percentage of each premium dollar the insurer spends on expenses* — overhead, marketing, and commissions. An insurer that spends 25 cents of each $1 of premium on expenses has a 25 percent expense ratio. (See **Combined ratio; Loss ratio**)

F

Facultative risks: See **Reinsurance policies**

FAIR Plans: After the urban demonstrations and riots of the mid-1960s, many inner city homeowners and business owners were unable to get property insurance in the regular market. In response, Fair Access to Insurance Requirements (FAIR) Plans were established in many states. These plans are *insurance pools that sell property insurance to people who can't buy it in the voluntary market because of their high exposure to risks over which they may have no control.* All FAIR Plan policies insure for losses from fire, vandalism, riot and windstorm. Some FAIR Plans also sell homeowners coverage.

About half the states operate FAIR Plans and require the participation of all insurers licensed to sell property coverage in the state. Any operating losses sustained by such an insurance pool are typically shared by its participants. In the 1980s, FAIR Plans started shrinking, because their policyholders increasingly were able to buy coverage in the regular insurance market. By 1990, FAIR Plan premiums accounted for 1.2 percent of property insurance premiums in states with Plans, down from 3.7 percent in 1972. (See **Assigned risk plans, Beach and Windstorm Plans**) Source for additional FAIR Plan information: Property Insurance Plans Service Office.

Farmowners-ranchowners insurance: *A package policy, like homeowners insurance, that protects the policyholder against a number of named perils and liabilities.* Typical farmowners and ranchowners policies cover a dwelling and its contents, as well as barns, stables and other structures.

Federal crime insurance: *Homeowners and business owners coverage for burglary and robbery losses provided by the federal government when the Federal Insurance Administration determines such coverage isn't available in the regular market.* Federal crime insurance is available in 14 states, the District of Columbia, the Virgin Islands and Puerto Rico. The policies are available for both businesses and individuals and sold through licensed insurance agents and brokers.

Federal Flood Insurance: See **Catastrophe/floods**

Federal Insurance Administration (FIA): The government *agency in charge of administering the Federal Flood Insurance Program and the Federal Crime Insurance Program.* The FIA does not regulate the insurance industry, which is state-regulated. (See **Regulation**)

Fidelity bond: *A form of protection which covers the policyholder for losses that he or she incurs as a result of fraudulent acts by persons named in the bond.* A fidelity bond typically indemnifies an insured business for losses caused by the dishonest acts of its employees.

File-and-use state: See **Rate regulation**

Financial guarantee insurance: *Covers losses from specific financial transactions.* The coverage guarantees investors in debt instruments they'll receive timely payment of principal and interest if there is default on the underlying debts. One of its uses, for example, is as a marketing tool for investment bankers who sell securities backed by loan portfolios, including credit card and auto loans.

There's a wealth of historical data on default rates on these loans, making it possible to price the coverage. In many cases, the insurer is also protected by over-collateralization of the securities — i.e., $1.15 in secured assets is used to back each $1 of the issue. (See **Municipal bond insurance**)

Financial responsibility law: *A state law requiring that all automobile drivers show proof that if involved in an auto accident, they can pay damages up to a specific minimum amount.* The requirement varies from state to state, and is usually met by carrying a minimum amount of auto liability insurance. (See **Auto policy; No-fault**)

Fire insurance: *Coverage protecting property against losses caused by fire or lightning.* Fire insurance is usually sold as part of a package policy (like homeowners or commercial multiperil) that also includes coverage for a variety of other named perils.

Floater: *Property insurance for items that are moved from location to location, covering losses wherever they occur.* It's typically bought to cover jewelry, furs and items whose full value isn't covered in standard homeowners policies.

Flood Insurance: See **Catastrophe/floods**

Foreign insurance company: In a given state, an insurer that is domiciled in another state is called a foreign insurer.

401(k) plan: *An employer-sponsored retirement savings plan funded by employee contributions, which may or may not be matched by the employer.* 401(k) plans are named for the section of the Internal Revenue Code that permits them. The law allows each employee to invest pre-tax dollars, up to a stated maximum each year. In 1993, the maximum amount is $8,994. It will increase in 1994. The employee's contribution is made through a payroll deduction from gross income, effectively reducing his or her income tax liability for the year. Many 401(k) plans allow the employee to manage his or her own account by selecting from a menu of investment choices. These typically include a fixed income account and stock and bond mutual funds. The 401(k) account's earnings are tax-deferred.

Depending on the plan design, employees may borrow from their 401(k) accounts (paying interest) without incurring taxes or penalty. But a withdrawal (as opposed to a loan) taken before the employee reaches age 59 and a half is subject to income tax and a 10 percent penalty. (See **Pension**) A 20 percent withholding tax applies to 401k plan payments for hardship withdrawals and when leaving a job, unless the money is sent directly to an IRA or another employer's retirement plan within 60 days.

Fraud: See **Insurance fraud**

Fronting: A *procedure in which a primary carrier acts as the insurer of record by issuing a policy, but then passes the entire risk to a reinsurer in exchange for a commission.*

Typically, the fronting insurer is licensed to do business in the particular state or country where the risk is located, and the reinsurer is not. Fronting is a service insurers provide to corporate policyholders with multinational operations. The reinsurer that ultimately assumes the risk is often a captive — an insurer wholly-owned by the corporate policyholder and created primarily to cover its parent's risks. Alternatively, the reinsurer is sometimes an independent carrier that cannot sell insurance directly in a particular country, because local coverage by law must be bought from a government-owned insurance company. (See **Captives; Reinsurance**)

General liability insurance: See **Commercial lines**

Glass insurance: *Coverage for glass breakage caused by all risks, subject to exclusions of war and fire.* This insurance can be bought for windows, art glass, structural glass, leaded glass, mirrors and more. Insurers agree to replace or repair broken glass or glass damaged by chemicals and to cover costs necessary to repair or replace damaged frames, to board up openings and to replace lettering and other decoration.

Group insurance: *A single policy covering a group of individuals — usually employees of the same company or members of the same association — and their dependents.* The group is covered under a master policy issued to the employer or association. About 90 percent of the Americans covered by commercial health insurance are insured under group policies, and more than 40 percent of life insurance in force in the United States is group coverage.

Guaranteed Investment Contracts (GICs): One of the life insurance industry's hottest new products in the early 1980s, GICS were sold to corporate profit-sharing 401(k) and pension plans. They *guarantee a specific return on invested capital over the life of the contract.* As interest rates fell later in the decade, some insurers sustained heavy losses on GICs that guaranteed higher rates than they could earn, and that permitted the investor to add to the original investment, at the original rate, for the life of the contract.

Other GICs were written to mature at the same time as the issuing insurers' short-term loans to real estate developers. When real estate values plummeted at the end of the 1980s, many developers were unable to repay their loans. Insurers that had intended the loans to pay off their five-year GICs had to extend new loans to the developers or foreclose on the properties, and use other monies to pay off the GICs.

Guaranteed replacement cost insurance: Insurance that pays the full cost of replacing damaged property, without a deduction for depreciation, and without a dollar limit. (See **Actual cash value**)

Guaranty associations: All 50 states, the District of Columbia, and Puerto Rico require licensed insurers to assume some of an insolvent insurance company's policyholder liabilities. Guaranty associations are *the mechanism by which solvent insurers bail out the policyholders of companies that fail.* The lines of insurance covered by guaranty associations and the maximum amount paid on any claim vary considerably from one state to another. In most states, life and health insurance lines and property/casualty lines are covered by two different guaranty associations.

Guaranty associations are sometimes referred to as guaranty funds. This is misleading, because insurers aren't required to pre-fund their guaranty obligations, except in New York State, which by law maintains a permanent property/casualty guaranty fund of not less than $150 million. In other states (and in New York's life/health guaranty association), insurers are assessed as needed to cover policyholder claims after an insolvency occurs. The assessment typically applies to all insurers doing business in a state in that line of insurance, regardless of where their home offices are located. Most state guaranty associations cover the claims of all policyholders who are state residents. (Source: National Conference of Insurance Guaranty Funds)

One obvious potential problem with this system is that a major insolvency could seriously weaken otherwise healthy insurers. Another is the difficulty of coordinating multi-state responses to an insolvency affecting consumers in many states.

Federal and state legislators and regulators and insurers have proposed a variety of ways to strengthen the guaranty association system. They fall into three basic categories: the establishment of federal solvency regulation; the creation of a national organization to handle insurer insolvencies and liquidations and coordinate multi-state response to a major insolvency; and the continuation of the present system but with stronger and more uniform state solvency laws. All three positions have advocates within the insurance industry. (See **Pension Benefit Guaranty Corporation; Insolvency; Risk-based capital**)

Guaranty funds: See **Guaranty associations**

Hard market: *A market environment in which insurance is expensive and in short supply; i.e., a seller's market.* (See **Property/casualty cycle**)

Health insurance: A generic term for many different forms of coverage. When people say health insurance, they usually mean coverage for medical expenses, such as fees for doctors or a hospital stay. But disability income (DI) insurance is also categorized as health insurance; DI replaces income lost when the insured is unable to work because of accident, illness, or pregnancy.

Health insurance benefits are not limited to medical expenses incurred as a result of illness or accident. Some policies, for example, routinely pay for normal pregnancy and well baby care. Moreover, because states mandate different health insurance benefits, some expenses — like wigs purchased by patients after undergoing radiation — may be covered, even though they are only tangentially related to illness. And other types of coverage — for example, auto insurance — may pay some medical expenses.

Health insurance claims are paid by:

- private, commercial insurers
- private, nonprofit insurers (e.g., some of the managed care plans)
- Blue Cross/Blue Shield plans (which differ from the two categories above in how they are treated for tax purposes)
- Self-insured plans

—Auto insurance
—Workers compensation insurance
—Disability insurance
—Medicare
—Medicaid
—CHAMPUS (the medical insurance system for the U.S. military)
—Veteran Affairs

Disability income insurance is provided by private commercial insurers and by government. (See **Disability insurance; Workers compensation; Health insurance/policies**)

Most Americans are covered for health insurance in group plans provided as an employee benefit at their jobs; most of the cost of this coverage typically is paid by employers. In 1990, a survey by the Health Insurance Association of America (HIAA) found that more than 82 million Americans were insured under group policies, and nearly 10 million people carried individual or family policies. (See **Consolidated Omnibus Budget Reconciliation Act**)

In 1992, more than half of all employees worked for companies that self-insured their health benefits — i.e., these employers used their own assets to pay claims. Self-insured plans typically are administered by insurance companies or third-party administrators. (See **Self-insurance**)

Health insurance/managed care: Managed care integrates the financing and delivery of health care to covered individuals. The employer and/or insurer arranges with selected providers to furnish comprehensive health care services to members of the insured group. The medical procedures and services performed by these providers are monitored for quality and cost. (See **Case management; Utilization review**)

Although managed care is still evolving, typical programs include:

- —Arrangements with medical providers to furnish a comprehensive set of health care services to covered individuals;
- —Explicit standards for the selection of health care providers;
- —Formal programs for ongoing quality assurance and utilization review by the employer or insurer; and
- —Significant financial incentives for members to use the providers and procedures covered by the plan.

Managed care plans attempt to assure quality and appropriateness of medical care through case management and utilization review, and by using primary care physicians as coordinators of patient care.

In the past 15 years, employers' efforts to control the cost of health benefits have been the driving force behind a shift toward managed care, and away from the traditional fee-for-service health care delivery and indemnity insurance systems.

In these traditional systems, an insured employee chooses his or her medical care providers from independent and unconnected doctors and hospitals. The providers bill for each service they perform. Indemnity insurance reimburses the patient based on what the insurer deems "reasonable and customary" fees — i.e., fees consistent with what other doctors and hospitals in the same area are charging for similar services. Typically, indemnity coverage reimburses the employee for 80 percent or more of what the insurer deems reasonable and customary.

Managed care is delivered by organizations such as Health Maintenance Organizations (HMOs) and Preferred Provider Organizations (PPOs). HMOs are organizations that provide services to an enrolled population for a fixed, prepaid, per capita fee. PPOs are networks of medical providers who charge on a fee-for-service basis, but are paid on a negotiated, discounted fee schedule.

Some employers have replaced indemnity coverage with managed care in their benefits plans. But more typically, employers continue to offer indemnity coverage benefits, along with managed care, as options among several types of coverage available in the benefits package. Employees are given a financial incentive to choose managed care.

Nationwide, 54 percent of employees covered by employer-sponsored health insurance were enrolled in HMOs, PPOs, or Point-of-Service (POS) health plans in 1991, while 46 percent were enrolled in conventional health plans. HMOs had the largest market share among managed care plans with 25 percent of the employer-based group health insurance market. PPOs followed with 22 percent of the market, and POS plans, which allow the employee to choose between in-network and out-of-network care each time they need medical care, represented 7 percent of the market.

Health insurance/policies: Basic health insurance provides benefits for conditions that require hospitalization. Typically, these benefits include room and board and other hospital services; surgery; physicians' nonsurgical services performed in a hospital; outpatient diagnostic X-ray and laboratory expense; and room and board in an extended care facility — i.e., a non-acute care facility providing skilled nursing services on an in-patient basis.

Benefits for surgery typically are listed in a policy schedule that itemizes specific types of procedures and the maximum benefit for each. Benefits for hospital room and board may be stated as a daily dollar amount or in terms of the hospital's daily rate for a semiprivate room.

— **Dental expense** insurance *covers dental services, sometimes, but not always including preventive care.*

— **Hospital indemnity policies** *pay a specified cash benefit for each day the insured person is hospitalized, up to a designated number of days.*

— **Long-term care insurance** *covers the cost of long-term custodial care in a nursing facility or at home,* following illness or injury or in old age, when the insured requires assistance to perform at least two of five basic activities of daily living: walking, eating, dressing, using the bathroom, and moving from one place to another. The cost of long-term custodial care isn't covered in any other form of health insurance policy. But it is paid by Medicaid for those who meet eligibility requirements, which vary from one state to another. In 1991, Medicaid paid for half of all Americans in nursing homes. (See **Medicaid**)

—**Major medical** coverage is *comprehensive health insurance, designed to pay the bills associated with serious illness both in and out of the hospital.* These policies typically pay most hospital expenses in full or at 80 percent. Medical expenses, however, are subject to both deductibles and coinsurance. Coinsurance typically applies up to a specified dollar amount in a given calendar year; after that is reached, covered benefits are paid in full. Major medical policies also have a lifetime dollar limit on benefits to be paid under the policy.

— **Medicare supplement** or Medigap policies *cover Medicare co-payments and deductibles, and sometimes pay benefits for items Medicare doesn't cover, like outpatient prescription drugs.*

Health insurance/profitability: Historically, health insurance company profitability depended on managing underwriting risk and expenses, and charging premiums that correctly gauged the future inflation of medical costs.

But underwriting — selecting whom to insure, based on risk characteristics — is fast disappearing from health insurance. Under community rating laws enacted by several states, insurers are required to accept all applicants for coverage, and to charge all applicants the same premium for the same coverage, regardless of their age or state of health. The premiums are based on a community rate determined by the health and demographic profile of a specified geographic region. Community rating can be modified by allowing insurers to take one or more demographic factors into account in setting rates.

Insurers have sought to control expenses by insuring big groups, which offer economies of scale. The market for small group and individual coverage has shrunk in the past 10 years. Insurers have tried to control medical care inflation through managed care, where they become part of the health care delivery system, through ownership or management of Health Maintenance Organizations and Preferred Provider Organizations. (See **Managed care** above)

Managed care has given insurers greater control of costs, but it has also reduced their profit margins because it is a very capital intensive business. It demands substantial investment in claims processing and administrative computer systems, and in building, maintaining and managing networks of health care providers.

Health insurance/reform: The primary goal of health care reform is clear: to address and resolve the two most serious problems of the present system — limited access and runaway costs.

National health care spending has climbed at twice the general inflation rate for more than a decade. In 1992, it accounted for 14 percent of Gross National Product, up from 13.2 percent in 1991. The U.S. Department of Commerce, the source for these numbers, expects medical spending to go up 12 percent to 15 percent a year over the next five years, unless significant changes are made in the health care system.

The United States spends more per capita on medical care than any other country in the world. But unlike most other industrialized nations, the United States doesn't provide universal access to health care. Some 37 million Americans — half of them employed people and their dependents — have no health insurance. Twenty-six percent of the nation's uninsured are children.

There are many underlying reasons for the enormous and growing cost of health care. Among them:

— At the end of 1990, most Americans had adequate health insurance coverage as an employee benefit, and most of its cost was paid by the employer. As a result, consumers have little incentive to comparison shop for medical care, or to learn the relative costs and benefits of the different medical treatments available, and reject those whose costs may far exceed potential benefits.

— There are no nationally accepted protocols for medical treatment to guide doctors and hospitals. One result is that treatments for the same disease vary widely from one region to another. It is estimated that 25 percent to 35 percent of all medical procedures are unnecessary.

— A fee-for-service delivery system does nothing to discourage doctors from ordering unnecessary treatments. Studies have shown that physicians who are paid on a fee-for-service basis order 50 percent more electrocardiograms and 40 percent more X-rays than those in managed care groups, for example.

Fear of malpractice suits is sometimes cited as the reason doctors order unnecessary medical tests. In a fee-for-service delivery system, however, it's impossible to tell how often testing is motivated by defensive medicine, rather than profit. (See **Malpractice insurance**)

— Medical technology has made it possible to prolong life in circumstances that couldn't have been foreseen even a decade ago — but at enormous cost. The cost and uses of this technology are a major contributor to medical inflation. The HIAA estimates that expensive new medical technologies account for 40 percent of the annual increase in health insurance premiums.

The Health Care Financing Administration (HCFA) data show that 29 percent of Medicare's budget is spent for health care of people over age 65 in their last year of life — more than half of this total in their last 30 days. Indeed, HCFA statistics show that Medicare reimbursements are consistently six times higher for people who die in a hospital than for hospitalized persons who recover.

This cost will grow significantly as the U.S. population ages. But the cost of procedures made possible by technology isn't confined to patients over age 65. Among the general population, for example, one in seven total health care dollars is spent on heroic measures during the last six months of someone's life. The nation has yet to address the ethical issues inherent in deciding under what circumstances life should be prolonged.

Many proposals have been made to change the current system. They include:

— Pay-or-Play, a system in which all employers would have to provide health insurance benefits. Those who didn't provide their own benefits plan would pay a payroll tax to support a public plan their employees could join.

— A system in which government is the sole buyer of health care, as is the case in many other industrialized countries. Canada, Britain, France, Denmark and Sweden, for example, all have different health care systems, but in each case, the government buys medical care for all citizens, with tax revenues.

The single payer approach frequently advocated in the United States is the Canadian system. Canadians can choose any doctor and hospital they wish; all medical providers operate in the private sector. The government pays for medical care, negotiates doctors' and hospitals' fees, and regulates hospitals' budgets and spending on medical technology. Private health insurance covers items government won't pay for, such as private hospital rooms and prescription drugs.

— Managed competition, which would build on our current job-based system of health benefits. Under the basic managed competition proposal, all Americans would be guaranteed a core package of health benefits, to be determined by the federal government. Benefits would be bought by big purchasing groups, from competing networks of managed care providers, whose services would be performed according to standards set by the government.

Each purchasing group would offer its members a choice of managed care plans. Small businesses and individuals would achieve the same marketplace clout as big firms, by buying their medical benefits as members of purchasing groups.

Workers aren't currently taxed on their health benefits, whose cost is deductible to employers. Under managed competition, one or both of these tax breaks might be limited to the cost of the basic benefits package. Self-employed and unemployed people would receive the same core set of benefits. In the case of the unemployed and the poor, the cost would be subsidized by the government.

Under some versions of the managed competition proposal, the federal government would set budget guidelines and price controls for medical providers.

Health insurance/reform in Oregon: In 1989 and 1991, the Oregon legislature passed a series of laws collectively known as the Oregon Health Plan. They expand Medicaid coverage to all state residents under the federal poverty level, mandate employment-based coverage, establish a high-risk insurance pool, and reform the small group insurance market to make affordable coverage available.

The state defines a basic benefit package for the Medicaid population. A similar package must be offered by every small business insurance carrier in the state. It is hoped that this package will also become the standard for other employment-based plans.

Oregon defines the Medicaid benefit package every two years. An independent commission of consumers and medical professionals ranks all health services according to their medical effectiveness and importance to the entire population. That information is gathered from community meetings and public hearings.

Legislators then "fund" the list from available resources, thus creating the basic benefit package. Services at the bottom of the list are not included if there is not enough money to do so.

The Clinton Administration approved the Oregon Health Plan in March 1993 after Oregon revised the health services list to avoid potential conflicts with the Americans with Disabilities Act.

The current list contains about 680 services, of which legislators hope to cover about 580 services. Diagnosis is covered. Primary and preventive care rank high and effective specialty and hospital services are also covered.

Illnesses whose treatment would probably not be covered include chronic bronchitis, viral hepatitis and strains and sprains. In general, the state would not reimburse for aggressive medical treatment in the final stage of a terminal illness. Doctors would not be reimbursed for trying to cure a cancer patient with less than a five percent chance of surviving. Instead, Oregon would provide comfort care such as pain management and hospice care.

The ultimate fate of the Oregon reforms is uncertain. They are the first substantive governmental attempt to ration health care according to explicit priorities and through an accountable process in order to provide a basic level of coverage for everyone.

Health maintenance organization: See **Health insurance/managed care**

Homeowners multiperil insurance: Americans spend about $20 billion a year on homeowners insurance. About 67 percent of Americans own their homes, and almost all of them have the coverage. Homeowners insurance is a *package policy, providing both property and personal liability insurance.*

The typical comprehensive policy covers the house, garage and other structures on the property — as well as personal property inside the house — against a wide variety of perils, including but not limited to fire, windstorm, riot or civil commotion, theft and vandalism, and accidental water damage from a plumbing, heating or air-conditioning system or domestic appliance. The number of covered perils depends on the breadth of the policy.

Trees and plants are not covered against windstorm damage. (Homeowners insurance will, however, cover damage to an insured structure caused by a tree that fell in a windstorm, and will pay to remove the tree.)

The typical homeowners policy includes theft coverage on personal property anywhere. That means policyholder belongings are insured against theft even when they're not inside the house. Coverage would apply to the theft of luggage, golf clubs, and other belongings while the policyholder was traveling, for example.

Homeowners insurance also provides additional living expenses to reimburse a policyholder for the cost of living elsewhere while his or her house is being repaired after a fire or other disaster.

The policy's liability insurance covers the homeowner and his or her dependents for accidental injuries they are found to have caused to third parties and/or their property. (See **Third party**)

Homeowners policy exclusions: Earthquake and flood damage caused by external flooding aren't covered by standard homeowners policies. These coverages are of interest only to the homeowners who, by virtue of where they live, are likeliest to suffer loss. Coverage can be separately purchased. Homeowners insurance also does not provide coverage for a nuclear accident. (See **Catas-**

trophe/earthquakes; Catastrophe/floods) The standard policy provides only limited coverage for items like jewelry, furs, silverware or stamp or coin collections. Again, additional coverage can be bought separately. (See **Floater**)

Homeowners policy limits of coverage: Most homes should be insured for replacement value — what it would cost to rebuild if destroyed. Replacement value shouldn't be confused with cash value, which usually is defined as replacement value less depreciation. Cash value and replacement value can be very different, depending on the age of a house and on what's happened to property values in the neighborhood. A large Victorian house with hand-carved banisters and ceiling moldings, for example, located in a neighborhood that has gone downhill for a decade, might cost considerably more to replace than its current selling price.

Many states have laws prohibiting insurers from refusing to sell coverage because of the age, sex, race, creed, color, national origin, marital status or occupation of the applicant. But in most states, insurers can refuse to sell replacement policies to applicants when the replacement value of the house is much greater than its current market value, or the property is particularly vulnerable to theft or damage. (See **Fair Plans; Redlining**)

Insurance agents, insurance company representatives and local real estate agents and appraisers are all good sources of information about the cost of rebuilding different types of houses, which is largely based on local construction costs. A good way to get a ballpark estimate of the cost of rebuilding a house is to calculate the square footage and multiply it by local building costs per square foot for that type of house. For example, if a house is 2,000 square feet and building costs in the community for that type of house are $80 per square foot, the cost to replace the house would be about $160,000.

To ensure that coverage is maintained at replacement value, many insurance companies sell homeowners policies that include an inflation guard clause. These policies automatically increase coverage on a regular basis to reflect current construction costs in the policyholder's area. Alternatively, the homeowner can buy a guaranteed replacement cost policy, which pays whatever it costs to rebuild a house as it was before the fire or other disaster — even if that cost exceeds the policy limit.

Homeowners policy premium discounts: Among the things that can reduce the premium are:

—A higher deductible

—More than one policy with the same carrier. Many companies that sell homeowners, auto and liability coverage offer discounts to people who keep two or more policies with them.

—Installation of protective devices like a smoke detector, sprinkler system or burglar alarm

—Being a nonsmoker

—Being retired

—Having a house constructed with fire-resistant building materials

Homeowners policy rates: The cost of homeowners insurance depends on the location, age and construction of the house, and what it would cost to replace. Building costs can vary dramatically from one part of the country to another.

Insurers maintain loss statistics by cities and neighborhoods. The quality of local fire and police protection is an important determinant of rates. Rural houses sometimes cost more to insure, even if they're less exposed to crime. The reason is that they don't have the protection of a full-time, professional fire department.

Hurricane: See **Catastrophe/hurricanes**

I

Incurred But Not Reported (IBNR) losses: Liability claims often aren't filed until years after a policy is sold. (The damage caused by a toxic substance, like asbestos, for example, may not be discovered until long after a person is exposed.) Liability insurers must therefore reserve for claims that have been incurred but haven't been reported. Only the passage of time reveals how accurately a company has estimated its IBNR losses. (See **Solvency; Balance sheet**)

Inflation guard clause or endorsement: *An addition to a homeowners insurance policy that automatically adjusts the dwelling limit when the policy is renewed, to reflect current construction costs in the area.*

Inland marine insurance: Nowadays, this coverage has very little to do with water. Years ago, when goods were mainly transported by water, the coverage referred to insurance for goods transported on the nation's inland waterways. Inland marine is *a broad category of coverage that includes insurance for articles in transit, as well as bridges, tunnels and other means of transportation and communication*. It also includes "floater" policies, which cover personal property, jewelry, furs, fine arts and other items whose value is above the standard homeowners policy limits for personal effects and household items.

Insolvency: Deciding whether an insurer is insolvent, i.e., *unable to pay its debts*, is far from simple, partly because insurance company solvency standards vary from state to state, and partly because the adequacy of reserves to pay future claims is a matter of opinion.

A state insurance regulatory body which deems a company in financial peril has a series of available legal options. It can take action to place the company in conservatorship, rehabilitation, or liquidation. (The difference between conservatorship and rehabilitation is one of degree: The state insurance department guides the operations of a company in conservatorship, and directs those of a company in rehabilitation.)

Typically, the first sign of problems is a company's failure to pass four or more of 11 financial tests regulators administer as a routine procedure. The insurance regulator can order the company to take whatever steps he or she thinks necessary to correct the problem, such as raising its rates, restructuring its investment portfolio, and increasing its capital.

These remedial actions usually aren't made public to avoid precipitating the equivalent of a run on the bank. If the company's situation doesn't improve, the regulator can seek a court order to place it in conservatorship or rehabilitation, and take additional steps to shore it up, such as suspending claims payments, placing a stay on lawsuits against the company, and looking for additional sources of capital.

The final step is liquidation, in which the insurance department sells the company's assets and settles its claims. The process of liquidation varies from state to state. In every state, however, the insurer's obligations to policyholders have first priority, ahead of all other creditors' claims for payment. (See **Solvency; Guaranty associations**)

Insurable risk: *Insurable risks are risks for which it is relatively easy to get insurance.* The insurable risk has as many of the following characteristics as possible:

1. The premium needed to insure the risk will be reasonable compared to the potential loss.
2. Many people who are exposed independently to the loss will buy the coverage. (See **Spread of risk**)
3. Their exposures have enough in common to make it possible to price the risk of loss. (See **Rate**)
4. The losses will be definite as to cause, time, place and amount. (Damage caused by environmental pollution is hard to insure in part because it lacks this characteristic.)
5. It's possible to calculate the expected loss for each insured during the policy period. (Some liability exposures, such as product liability and medical malpractice liability, are difficult to insure because they lack this characteristic. Claims may not be filed until long after the policy period is ended.)
6. The loss will be accidental from the viewpoint of the insured.

Insurance: The idea is simple: *a system to make financial loss more affordable by transferring it from individuals to large groups.* One family's house burns down, and the family is financially wiped out. The insurance system shrinks the individual family's loss by pooling the risks of hundreds of thousands of families: In exchange for a premium, each family transfers its risk of loss to the pool, through the mediation of the insurer. The premium each family pays is small compared to the potential loss it's insuring. But the insurer can afford to pay for all the covered losses, if it has charged premiums to the pool of homeowners that are commensurate with the risk of loss, and if all the houses it covers don't burn down at the same time. (See **Rate; Spread of risk**)

Insurance company: Insurance companies vary by corporate structure, by the types of insurance they sell, and by the marketing methods they employ.

There are two basic insurance company structures: mutual and stock. A mutual company is owned by its policyholders. Part of its profit is returned to policyholders in the form of dividends. The rest is retained by the insurer as a surplus cushion to protect policyholders if the company experiences larger-than-expected insurance or investment losses.

A stock company is owned by its stockholders, who share its profits in earnings distributions and increases in the value of its stock.

Some insurers are multi-line companies, which means they sell all types of property, casualty, life and health insurance. But most insurance companies sell either property and casualty coverage, or life and health insurance. Even multi-line companies sell property/casualty coverage and life and health coverage out of separate subsidiaries.

Insurers market their products through a sales force of agents. Companies that sell coverage through independent agents — agents who don't work exclusively for one company, but typically represent several insurers — are called agency companies. Companies that sell coverage through a sales force that works exclusively for them are known as direct companies, because they market directly to the public rather than through an independent intermediary.

Insurance company size: This can be measured by assets; by premiums written — i.e., by the premiums collected from policyholders; or by net premiums — i.e., the amount of premium retained by the insurer after the purchase of reinsurance; or by the amount of insurance in force — i.e., the face amount of coverage the company has sold. Insurance in force typically is a measure of life insurance companies.

Insurance fraud: *1. Intentional lying or concealment by policyholders to obtain payment of an insurance claim that would otherwise not be paid. 2. Lying or misrepresentation by insurance company managers, employees, agents and brokers for their personal enrichment.*

Fraudulent claims are difficult to quantify because by their nature they are concealed, but they are generally conceded to represent a substantial piece of insurance losses. In property/casualty insurance, fraudulent claims are estimated to account for 10 percent of all claims dollars, costing more than $17 billion a year. In health care, they are estimated to cost more than $50 billion a year.

Fraudulent activity includes inflating actual claims, filing multiple claims for the same accident, and submitting claims for injuries that never happened. Fraud is committed by individuals and by corporations, and often is abetted by professionals, including doctors and lawyers, who provide services to claimants.

Fraud committed by individuals includes acts like abandoning an unwanted car in a high-crime neighborhood and then filing an insurance claim for theft. Fraud committed by corporations includes employers who misrepresent their payroll or the kind of work done by their employees in order to lower their workers compensation premiums.

Since the mid-1980s, the escalating cost of insurance and the growth of organized insurance fraud have led insurers and government to fight fraud much more aggressively than in the past.

Many states have passed laws specifically defining the crime of insurance fraud or raising it from a misdemeanor to a felony. An increasing number of insurance departments now have fraud bureaus, which specialize in investigating cases in order to bring them to trial. And there has been a dramatic increase in the number of insurance companies with special investigative units charged with identifying and investigating suspicious claims.

For many years, the industry's most active anti-fraud organizations have been the Insurance Crime Prevention Institute and the National Auto Theft Bureau. In 1992, they were merged into the National Insurance Crime Bureau (NICB). NICB played a key role in finding the van used in the 1993 bombing of New York City's World Trade Center.

Insurance industry: Although consumers typically think of insurers as being part of one industry, there are in reality three distinct insurance industries, each selling different products and subject to different regulations and market forces. They are:

— **Life and health insurance.** At year-end 1991, there were 2,105 life insurers in the United States, with $1.6 trillion in assets. Collectively, these companies had $9.9 billion of life insurance in force, and responsibility for nearly $746 billion in pension and retirement money. In 1993, there were an estimated 1,500 commercial health insurance companies in the United States, covering more than 86 million Americans with group or individual insurance policies.

—**Property/casualty insurance.** In 1992, there were an estimated 3,900 property/casualty insurers in the United States, and they held more than $601 billion in assets.

— **Reinsurance.** Most large insurers engage in some reinsurance business, but relatively few are primarily engaged in reinsurance. These companies are called professional reinsurers. At year-end 1991, the insurance rating agency A.M. Best & Co. listed 139 professional reinsurers in the United States, with $63.1 billion in assets. Twenty of these companies did 70 percent of the professional reinsurance business in the United States.

But reinsurance is very much an international business. At year-end 1991, there were about 2,200 reinsurance companies in

100 countries outside the United States. American insurance companies rely on foreign as well as domestic reinsurance markets. Approximately 40 percent of U.S. exposures are reinsured by European, Japanese and other non-U.S. reinsurers. (See **Property/casualty insurance**; **Life insurance**; **Health insurance**; **Reinsurance**; **Surety bond**)

Insurance industry investments: Matching assets to liabilities is a cornerstone of insurance company investing. Property/casualty company liabilities are highly unpredictable: A sudden catastrophe might require immediate loss payments. Liquidity is therefore a major consideration in property/casualty insurers' investments. Most of their assets are invested in government, corporate and utility bonds and high grade stocks. Less than 2 percent of property/casualty industry assets are in real estate; less than 1 percent are in junk bonds.

Life insurers have much more predictable future costs than property/casualty carriers and offset their liabilities with long-term investments in fixed income securities, mortgages and real estate. But the life insurance industry has become more vulnerable to short-term economic changes in the past 15 years, as its product mix and customer attitudes have changed. (See **Life insurance/profitability**)

Interest rates, and consumer awareness of them, rose dramatically during the late 1970s and early 1980s. In response to these changes, life insurers introduced interest-sensitive products. Their traditional long-term investments couldn't earn enough to cover the higher rates guaranteed on the new policies. Some companies reached for higher yields by investing in junk bonds and riskier mortgages. (See **Guaranteed Investment Contracts; Junk bonds; Real estate investments; Early warning system**)

Insurance pool: A group of insurance companies that pledge assets to enable them together to provide an amount of insurance substantially more than can be provided by individual companies. (See **Catastrophe/nuclear accidents**)

Insurance-to-value: Insurance written in an amount approximating the value of the insured property. **(See Property/casualty insurance; Life insurance; Health insurance; Reinsurance; Surety bond**)

Insured: The policyholder is the insured.

Investment income: Insurers have two major sources of income — underwriting (i.e., premium income less claims and expenses) and the *investment earnings of assets.* Investment income is critical to the financial stability of both property/casualty and life insurers. For property/casualty companies, investment earnings help to balance underwriting losses. (Investment income is what enables insurers to stay profitable during years of heavy and unexpected losses caused by hurricanes, earthquakes and other natural catastrophes, for example.)

For life insurers, investment earnings build policy cash reserves, and thus are an integral part of cash value life insurance policies, which consist of an investment account as well as an insurance benefit. (See **Life insurance; Underwriting income; Real estate investments)**

J

Joint Underwriting Association (JUA): *A combination of several insurers, who join together to provide coverage for a particular type of risk or size of exposure.* Joint underwriting associations mandated by state law to provide auto insurance to drivers unable to obtain it in the regular market are pooling mechanisms, in which all insurers doing business in the state share the premiums, and profits or losses of risks assumed by the pool. Typically several insurers agree for a fee to issue and service policies underwritten by the pool.

An alternative method of providing insurance to drivers unable to buy it in the voluntary market is through state-mandated assigned risk plans. Again, participation of all insurers is required. But the assigned risk plan generally is administered through an office created or supported by the state. This office distributes applications for coverage to all insurers that offer auto liability insurance in the state, in proportion to the amount of their voluntary business.

Junk bonds: Junk bonds are corporate bonds with credit ratings of BB or less. Because their issuers have a higher perceived risk of default, junk bonds pay a higher yield than investment grade bonds. One reason buyers are willing to assume this greater credit risk is that default rates on non-investment grade bonds as a group historically haven't been as bad as commonly perceived.

All bonds also involve market risk — the risk that the bonds will have to be sold at a time when their market value is severely diminished. That's what several life insurers were forced to do when the 1990 junk bond market crash precipitated a consumer crisis of confidence. In the equivalent of a run on the bank, consumers with redeemable life insurance policies cashed out of companies whose investments they believed were shaky. This contributed to at least two of the seven major life insurer insolvencies of 1991 — those of Executive Life Insurance Co. and Mutual Benefit Life Insurance Co.

Kidnap/ransom insurance: *Coverage up to specific limits for ransom demanded by kidnappers for the release of an individual held against his will.* Kidnap/ransom coverage typically is bought by big international corporations to cover their employees. Most policies have large deductibles and exclude coverage in specified geographic areas. Some policies require that the policyholder not reveal the policy's existence.

L

Liability insurance: *Insurance for money the policyholder is legally obligated to pay because of bodily injury or property damage caused to another person and covered in the policy.*

Life insurance: *Protection against the death of the insured person in the form of payment to a designated beneficiary, typically a family member or business.* The policy payment is called a death benefit.

Life insurance products: There are only two basic types of life insurance — term and cash value coverage. Cash value policies include whole life, universal life, variable life, and variable/universal life insurance.

Term insurance is pure protection against premature death. A term policy pays its benefit only when an insured dies within a specified period. If the insured person dies while the policy is in force, the designated beneficiary receives the death benefit. If the insured person lives past the designated term, the policy ends and the beneficiary receives nothing. Renewable term life insurance includes a provision that gives the policyholder the right to renew the insurance coverage at the end of the specified term without submitting evidence of insurability. Term insurance premiums are low for young people, and gradually go up as the insured person ages and his or her mortality risk increases.

Cash value insurance combines protection with a savings or investment feature. Cash value policies are designed to last the policyholder's lifetime and are called permanent insurance. Cash value premiums are three to eight times greater than the initial term premium for the same amount of coverage; unlike term premiums, they remain level for the life of the policy. Cash value premiums fund the cost of insurance and the savings or investment account, which can be invested in a variety of ways, depending on the type of cash value policy chosen.

The cash value accumulates tax-deferred and the policyholder can borrow it (up to a limit specified in the policy) without incurring tax liability. The death benefit is reduced by the amount of any policy loans outstanding plus interest when the insured dies. Cash value life insurance products are often used as an investment for retirement. (See **Annuity; Pension**)

Life insurance is sold in both individual and group policies. The latter typically are offered as an employee benefit, or by associations to their members. (See **Accelerated death benefits; Credit insurance; Disability insurance; Whole life insurance; Variable life insurance; Universal life insurance**)

Life insurance/profitability: Life insurance company profitability depends on the management of underwriting risk, investment risk and expenses.

Underwriting is the analysis of the risk factors that affect life expectancy, to determine whether to cover the applicant, and at what price. The risk factors include the applicant's age, gender, occupation and state of health. Only about 3 percent of all life insurance applications are rejected. Underwriting risk has been minimized by steadily improving mortality throughout the twentieth century.

But expense management and investment management have become more important and complex since the 1980s, when new policies that pay a market rate of interest reduced the industry's profit margins.

Life insurance sales and marketing costs have always been high. Insurers typically don't start making a profit on a policy until seven years after it is sold. Because the cost of selling a policy is so high, a company's lapse ratio — the percentage of policies dropped by the purchaser after one or two years — is a key determinant of profitability. At the same time, the more accurately a company estimates its future lapse ratios, the more competitively it can price products without sacrificing profit.

The universal and interest-sensitive whole life policies introduced in the 1980s are bought by interest-sensitive customers. They entail liquidity risk for insurers — the risk that consumers will cash out of their policies in response to a change in interest rates, forcing the insurer to sell underlying investments at a loss. Many insurers have minimized this risk with policy surrender fees. (See **Insurance industry investments**)

Lloyd's of London: The original Lloyd's was a seventeenth century London coffee house patronized by shipowners, who insured each others' hulls and cargoes as a sideline. Edward Lloyd, who owned the coffee house, supplied his customers with pens and ink, and sold coffee — not insurance.

Lloyd's of London today is still a gathering place for underwriters, not an insurance company. Lloyd's is a marketplace, made up of hundreds of underwriting syndicates, each of them in effect a mini-insurer. As a corporate entity, Lloyd's sets standards for its members, but doesn't issue policies. (Bruce Springsteen's voice, for example, was not insured *by* Lloyd's; it was insured *at* Lloyd's.)

Each syndicate is managed by an underwriter who decides which risks to accept. Typically, a risk underwritten at Lloyd's will be shared by many syndicates. The number of individual investors in an underwriting syndicate can vary from a few to hundreds. These investors, or members of Lloyd's, are also known as "names." The Lloyd's market is a major international reinsurer. American insurers' involvement with Lloyd's is primarily as buyers of reinsurance. Where a Lloyd's syndicate is the primary insurer of a large risk, it may choose to limit its involvement by reinsuring in the United States.

Lloyds: *Groups of individuals, called syndicates (not insurance companies) that assume liability through an underwriter.* Each individual independently and personally assumes a proportionate part of the risk accepted by the underwriter. American Lloyds are named after but have no connection with Lloyd's of London, and account for only a miniscule part of the property/casualty insurance market in the United States.

Long-term care insurance: See **Health insurance/policies**

Loss: In insurance terms, *a reduction in the quantity or value of a property.* Also, the basis on which an insurance claim is submitted.

Loss-of-use coverage: See **Renters insurance**

Loss ratio: The percentage of each premium dollar an insurer spends on claims. An insurer with a 92 percent loss ratio spends 92 cents of each $1 of premium on claims. (See **Combined ratio; Expense ratio**)

Loss reserves: Loss reserves are a liability on the insurer's balance sheet, not an actual fund of money. Loss reserves represent *the company's best estimate of what it will pay for claims*, an estimate that is periodically readjusted. Loss reserves can only be set up for events that have occurred, or are presumed to have occurred. (See **Capital & surplus; Solvency; Incurred But Not Reported losses**)

Malpractice insurance: *A professional liability coverage that insures physicians, lawyers and other specialists against suits alleging their negligence and/or errors and omissions have harmed their clients.* In the early 1970s, worsening losses in medical malpractice caused several insurers to stop selling the coverage, while those that stayed in the market sharply raised their rates. One result of this "medical malpractice crisis" was the formation of doctor-owned malpractice insurance companies. By the end of the 1980s, these companies wrote well over 40 percent of the medical malpractice coverage sold in the United States.

The reasons for the increased frequency of medical malpractice claims and the surge in the size of awards in the early 1970s are unclear. Also unclear is the extent to which the practice of defensive medicine, including diagnostic tests, may have added to the cost of health care. Estimates of the cost of defensive medicine range from $5 billion to as much as $15 billion. But some health care analysts and consumer groups point out that because most physicians are compensated on a fee-for-service basis, the increase in diagnostic tests may be attributable to a profit motive as well as to defensive medicine.

Managed Care: See **Health insurance**

Manual: A book published by an insurance or bonding company, a rating association or bureau, giving rates, classifications, and underwriting rules.

Marine insurance: *Coverage for goods in transit, and for the vehicles that transport them, on waterways, over land and in the air.* Ocean marine insurance covers damage or destruction of a ship's hull and cargo as the result of an insured peril. Insured perils include collision of the ship with another object; sinking, capsizing, or being stranded; fire; piracy; and jettisoning cargo to save other property. Excluded are damages that result from wear and tear, dampness, mold, and war. (See **War risk**)

McCarran-Ferguson: This is the *federal law* (1945) *in which* Congress declared that the states would continue to regulate the insurance business. As a result, *insurers are granted a limited exemption to federal antitrust legislation*. McCarran-Ferguson states that federal antitrust laws are applicable to the insurance business "to the extent that such business is not regulated by state law." (See **Antitrust laws; Regulation**)

Medicaid: A joint federal/state public assistance program created in 1965 for people whose income and resources are insufficient to pay for health care. Medicaid is administered by the states. Benefits and eligibility vary widely from one state to another.

Medical payments insurance: A coverage, available in various liability insurance policies, in which the insurer agrees to reimburse the insured and others, without regard for the insured's liability, for medical or funeral expenses incurred as the result of bodily injury or death by accident under specified conditions.

Medicare: A federal program for people ages 65 or older that pays part of the costs associated with hospitalization, surgery, doctors' bills, home health care, and skilled-nursing care. Everyone who reaches age 65 and is eligible for Social Security or Railroad Retirement is eligible for Medicare. Certain people under 65 who are disabled or who suffer from end-stage renal disease are also eligible. (See **Health insurance**)

Medigap/MedSup: Because Medicare does not cover all expenses, private insurers sell MedSup (or Medigap) *policies to supplement federal insurance benefits.* (See **Health insurance**)

Multiperil policy: *A package policy which provides coverage against several different perils.* Homeowners insurance and auto insurance are both multiperil policies.

Municipal bond insurance: This coverage *guarantees bondholders timely payment of interest and principal even if the issuer of the bonds defaults.* It's marketed by top-rated insurance companies. (See **Rating agencies**) A municipality that buys the insurance takes on the Triple-A credit rating of the insurance company selling it, and can thus raise money at lower interest rates.

Mutual insurance company: See **Insurance company**

N

Named perils: *Perils specified in a policy as those against which the policyholder is insured.*

National flood insurance program: See **Catastrophe/floods**

No-fault: No-fault is *a system in which each driver's auto insurance coverage pays for his or her own injuries, no matter who caused the accident.* Currently, 14 states and Puerto Rico have some form of no-fault law.

No-fault laws are intended to promote faster, more equitable reimbursement of expenses to accident victims, and at the same time lower the cost of coverage by reducing litigation. Under no-fault, reimbursement of victims isn't delayed until blame can be assigned. The trade-off is that drivers forfeit the right to sue except in serious injury cases.

By contrast, in states that don't have no-fault laws, damages are paid by the insurance of the person who is found to be at fault. In some states, the extent of the reimbursement depends on the degrees of fault attributed to the various parties involved. In a state that doesn't have no-fault, auto insurance buyers are essentially buying coverage to protect someone else. In no-fault states, the insurance buyer's policy protects the policyholder.

State no-fault laws vary primarily in the breadth of coverage they require, and in how they define an injury serious enough to warrant a lawsuit for additional damages. The laws that most effectively hold insurance costs down are those mandating modest coverage and barring suits for additional damages except in cases of permanent injury or death.

Non-admitted assets: See **Assets**

Non-admitted insurer: Insurers are licensed by the states. States call insurers they haven't licensed — but which may be licensed in other states — "non-admitted" companies. Some states permit non-admitted insurers to sell coverage that's unavailable from licensed companies within their borders. This kind of coverage is called "excess and surplus lines insurance."

Each state has its own rules for non-admitted carriers.

Non-admitted insurers range from long-established and well-capitalized entities like Lloyd's of London to small off-shore companies with little if any capitalization. Poorly-capitalized off-shore companies operating as non-admitted carriers are a much bigger problem than they were decades ago, in part because the nature of the excess and surplus lines market has changed.

As its name suggests, excess and surplus coverage historically was esoteric rather than standard insurance. It typically was bought by sophisticated policyholders. Examples of excess and surplus coverage include the policies that entertainment and promotion companies buy to cover rock concerts, and corporate coverages such as kidnap/ransom insurance and pollution liability insurance.

But as markets for health and auto insurance have become financially troubled, standard coverages have become scarce and expensive. Non-admitted insurers have found many customers for basic coverage, especially in the nation's inner cities. In the aftermath of the 1992 rioting in Los Angeles, it became clear that uncapitalized non-admitted carriers had sold millions of dollars of worthless insurance to South Central property owners.

Nursing home insurance: See **Health insurance policies/long-term care insurance**

Occupational disease: *Any abnormal condition or disorder, other than one resulting from an occupational injury, caused by exposure to factors associated with employment.* Most illnesses relating to workplace activity, like contact dermatitis and carpal tunnel syndrome, are easy to identify. Others, such as long-term latent illnesses caused by exposure to carcinogens, can be more difficult to relate to the workplace.

Ocean marine insurance: *Coverage on all types of vessels, for property damage to the vessel and cargo, and liabilities connected with them.* War risk is excluded under standard policies, but may be purchased separately. (See **Marine insurance; War risk**)

Open competition states: See **Rate regulation**

Ordinary life insurance: *A life insurance policy that is designed to remain in force for the policyholder's lifetime.* By contrast, term life insurance provides coverage for a specified number of years, and when it is renewable, the renewals are also for a specified amount of time.

P

Package policy: *A single insurance policy that combines several coverages once sold separately*. Homeowners insurance and commercial multiperil insurance are both package policies, combining property, liability and theft coverages originally sold as separate policies.

Pay-at-the-Pump: Refers to proposals to create *a system in which auto insurance premiums would be paid to state governments through a per-gallon surcharge on gasoline.* To ensure that drivers don't pay the same premiums regardless of their track records, this system would incorporate underwriting criteria currently used to set rates — like a driver's age and accident record — into driver licensing fees by use of surcharges and fines. The states would contract with private insurers to administer the claims handling of the program. The insurance industry has opposed Pay-at-the Pump, on several grounds, among them that it would unfairly penalize families with large cars or vans that get few miles to the gallon, that it would deny consumers the right to choose their own insurance carrier, and that it would create an enormous and expensive state bureaucracy. (Under some proposals, consumers might be able to choose their own carrier if they paid an extra fee.)

Pension: By the end of 1991, Americans had more than $2 trillion in private pension plans — *programs to provide employees with retirement income after they meet minimum age and service requirements*. Nearly $746 billion of this money was held by life insurers — up from $193 billion in 1981.

The predominant source of revenue for the life insurance business is in investment products for retirement, rather than insuring against premature death. (See **Life insurance**)

If they have contributed toward their pension, employees are automatically entitled to get back ("vested in") their own contributions to a pension plan when they retire. Under the Employee Retirement Income Security Act (ERISA) of 1974, an employee must be vested in contributions made by the employer in his or her behalf after completing five years of service. Alternatively, the employee may become 20 percent vested in employer contributions after three years of service, increase vesting by 20 percent annually thereafter, and be fully vested at the end of seven years of service.

Responsibility for pension savings increasingly has shifted from employers to employees during the past 10 years. Employer-funded "defined benefit" plans that promise workers a specific retirement income now account for less than 20 percent of all pension plans. They've been replaced by "defined contribution" plans like 401(k)s, employee stock ownership and profit-sharing plans — plans financed by employee contributions that may or may not be matched by the employer.

No retirement benefit is guaranteed in defined contribution plans, and participation frequently is voluntary. Employees make their own investment choices from a menu provided by the employer. Stock and bond mutual funds, money market funds, annuities, and guaranteed investment contracts are often among these choices. (See **Life insurance; Guaranteed Investment Contracts**)

Pension Benefit Guaranty Corporation (PBGC): A federal government fund created by the Employee Retirement Income Security Act (ERISA) of 1974. It guarantees that the vested benefits of employees whose pension plans have been terminated will be paid as they come due. (Coverage is not unlimited. The PBGC pays benefits only up to specified amounts.)

The PBGC guarantees only "defined benefit" pension plans — i.e., plans that promise retirees a specific monthly benefit based on their earnings. It does not cover "defined contribution plans" like 401(k)s, employee stock ownership and profit-sharing plans. The PBGC is financed by annual premiums paid by employers, and based on the number of employees covered in their pension plans.

Peril: *A specific risk covered by an insurance policy*, such as fire, windstorm, or theft. A homeowners policy is called a multiperil policy because it covers the policyholder against a wide number of specific risks. A named-peril policy covers the insured only against risks specified in the policy. By contrast, an all-risk policy automatically covers all causes of loss except those that are specifically excluded.

Personal article floater: *A policy or an addition to a policy, used to cover personal valuables, such as furs and jewelry.*

Personal lines: *Property/casualty insurance products that are designed for and bought by individuals.* The main personal lines coverages are automobile and homeowners. (See **Auto, Homeowners multiperil, Renters insurance**)

Point-of-Service plan: See **Health insurance/managed care**

Policy: *A written contract for insurance between the insurance company and the policyholder* stating which perils or damages are covered, and which are not.

Policyholders' surplus: *The amount of money remaining after an insurer's liabilities are subtracted from its assets.* Policyholders' surplus is a financial cushion protecting a company's policyholders against unexpected or catastrophic losses.

Political risk insurance: *Coverage for businesses operating abroad, against loss due to political upheavals, including war, revolution, confiscation of property, and incontrovertibility of local currency.*

Pollution insurance: Insurance *policies specifically covering losses and liabilities arising from damages caused by pollution*, for sites that have been inspected and found to be uncontaminated. Pollution coverage is written on a claims-made basis; that is, the policies pay only claims presented to the insurer during the term of the policy or within a specific time frame after its expiration.

Since 1986, comprehensive general liability policies have excluded coverage for pollution. General liability policies typically are occurrence policies — i.e., they pay claims arising out of incidents that occurred during the policy term, even if these claims are not filed until many years later.

Insurers and their corporate policyholders for the past 20 years have been engaged in a still unresolved legal battle as to whether or not pre-1973 general liability policies cover pollution damages that have become apparent since they were sold — and if so, what damages are and what damages are not covered. (See **Commercial general liability insurance; Superfund**)

Pool: *A group of insurers or reinsurers that together underwrite a particular risk, sharing premiums, losses and expenses according to a predetermined agreement.* Typically, the risk or risks shared by a pool are too big to be borne by a single carrier, such as super tankers and nuclear power plants. Some insurance pools are formed voluntarily by insurers. Others are mandated by the state to cover risks that cannot obtain coverage in the voluntary market. (See **Assigned risk plans; Beach and Windstorm Plans; FAIR Plans**)

Preferred Provider Organization: See **Health insurance/managed care**

Premium: *The price of an insurance policy, typically charged annually or semiannually.* (See **Direct premiums; Earned premium; Unearned premium**)

Premium tax: *A state tax on premiums paid by its residents and businesses, collected by insurers.* Companies that self-insure avoid this tax. (See **Self-insurance**)

Prior approval states: See **Rate regulation**

Product liability: A section of tort *law that determines who may sue and who may be sued for damages when a defective product injures someone.* There are currently no uniform federal laws governing manufacturers' liability. A manufacturer normally is liable when a defective product injures someone. Under the doctrine of strict liability, an injured person does not have to show negligence on the part of the manufacturer. It's sufficient to show that the product is defective and caused the injury. (See **Commercial lines**)

Professional liability: See **Commercial lines**

Profitability: See **Property/casualty insurance/profitability; Life insurance/profitability; Health insurance/profitability; Underwriting income; Investment income; Loss ratio; Expense ratio; Combined ratio**

Property/casualty cycle: Since the 1920s, the property/casualty business has been cyclical, alternating between periods of profit and loss. Periods of underwriting profit result in increased competition: Insurers lower their premiums to protect or to gain market share. As a result, the insurance market turns "soft" — i.e., it becomes a buyer's market. Lower premiums eventually result in underwriting losses, eventually depleting insurance industry capital, and reducing the supply of insurance. The market thus turns "hard." In a "hard" market, rates rise significantly and often there are shortages of insurance.

Since the 1970s, soft markets have lasted longer, and hard markets have been of briefer duration than in the past.

One development that has prolonged soft markets in the past 20 years is corporate self-insurance. Historically, the property/casualty cycle has resulted from changes in the supply of insurance, which is plentiful during periods of underwriting profit (or extremely high interest rates) and scarce after prolonged underwriting losses have depleted industry capital. Demand for product remained relatively stable.

But since the 1970s, self-insurance has reduced corporate demand for insurance, just as the ability to issue commercial paper reduced corporate reliance on bank loans. By the end of the 1980s, captives and other forms of self-insurance accounted for about one-third of U.S. insurance premiums. (See **Capacity; Captives**)

Property/casualty insurance: Property insurance covers damage to or loss of the policyholder's property. The terms casualty and liability insurance often are used interchangeably; both cover the policyholder's legal liability for damages caused to other persons and/or their property — i.e., damage to third parties, which is why casualty insurance is sometimes called third-party coverage. But casualty insurance has a broader meaning than liability insurance, because it also encompasses plate glass, burglary, theft and workers compensation coverages.

Property/casualty insurance/profitability: For property/casualty insurers, profitability depends on accurate pricing of policies and reserving for future claims, and on skillful expense management. The harder it is to price risks accurately — whether because of regulatory constraints on premium increases, marketplace competition, or the difficulty of estimating future losses — the more important it becomes to control expenses.

Liability insurance is potentially more profitable than property insurance, but also riskier. Liability claims often aren't filed until years after a policy is written. (An error in medical procedure, for example, may not be detected until long after the procedure is carried out.) This means the insurer can invest the premium for much longer, maximizing investment income. But it also makes pricing policies much more difficult, because it's hard to estimate what losses will be years into the future.

Accurate reserving is much easier on property coverages, because losses are known very soon: A house either burns down during the policy year or it doesn't. If it does, the claim is filed almost immediately. Property coverage is described as having "a short tail."

Liability coverage has "a long tail." Insurers must reserve for **Incurred But Not Reported (IBNR) losses** — losses that may not be known for years and may be dramatically affected by inflation and changing social attitudes and legislation. The biggest risk faced by property/casualty insurers is that their reserves will prove inadequate in the face of inflation, court awards, environmental claims, and natural disasters. (See **Claims-made policy**)

Proposition 103: This California referendum calling for a statewide, arbitrary rollback of auto insurance rates was the 1980s' most dramatic manifestation of consumer anger about the high cost of auto insurance. The state's difficulties in implementing Proposition 103 since its passage serve equally well to illustrate the complexity of auto insurance market problems.

Proposition 103 was approved by California voters by a 51 percent to 49 percent vote on November 8, 1988.

The law mandated a 20 percent insurance rate rollback from November 1987 levels, plus an additional 20 percent discount for "good drivers." (Good drivers were defined as those with not more than one conviction for a moving violation.) The law was challenged by insurers, but in essence upheld by the California Supreme Court in 1989. However, the court added the proviso that any rate rollback must allow insurance companies to make "a fair rate of return."

In mid-1993, the California insurance department had not yet created a court-approved rate rollback formula that encompassed both the rollbacks it required and this Supreme Court directive. Insurers were operating under so-called emergency regulations which require them to use the rating plans that they devised earlier to implement the mandates of Proposition 103.

R

Rate: *A rate is the cost of a unit of insurance (usually $1,000 worth).* Insurance rates are based on historical loss experience for similar risks. What a driver pays for auto insurance, for example, is based in part on past loss experience with drivers the same age, sex, and marital status, with similar driving records, and on experience with the same make and model car. The final premium also includes factors for future inflation, sales commissions, administrative expenses and profit.

State insurance regulators are responsible for making sure that insurance rates are adequate to cover losses, but not unreasonably high or unfairly discriminatory — i.e., individuals and groups with the same risk characteristics must be offered similar rates. (See **Regulation**)

Rate regulation: There are two basic systems of rate regulation — open competition and prior approval. In prior approval states, insurance companies must file proposed rate changes with the state regulator before putting them into effect. The ratings then may be approved or disapproved.

In open competition states, insurance companies may put new rates into effect without prior approval. But the insurance commissioner generally reserves the right to disallow rates within a certain period of time, if they are deemed inconsistent with the principles of regulation — i.e., that rates be adequate, reasonable, and not unfairly discriminatory. (In a file-and-use state, insurers must file rate changes, but don't have to wait for approval to put them into effect.)

Big insurers typically file their own rates. Smaller companies often use claims data filed on their behalf by statistical bureaus — industry associations that gather statistical data and prepare policy forms for their members. (See **Statistical data**)

Rate suppression: *The setting of insurance rates by government regulators at levels below their true economic cost.* The two major lines of coverage most affected by rate suppression are private passenger auto insurance and workers compensation, which together accounted for 50 percent of the property/casualty industry's premium volume in 1990.

In these two lines of coverage, claim costs have risen faster than in all other lines of property/casualty insurance combined; and in both workers compensation and private passenger auto insurance, claim costs have risen faster than premiums. (See **Auto insurance**; **Workers compensation**)

Rating agencies: Four major credit agencies rate insurers' financial strength and ability to meet their claims obligations. These privately owned agencies are A.M. Best Co., Standard & Poor's Corp., Moody's Investors Service Inc. and Duff & Phelps Inc. Best specializes in the insurance industry and has been rating insurers since 1899. S&P, Moody's and Duff & Phelps are bond-rating agencies that have branched into rating insurers in the past decade.

Each agency has its own methods. Among the factors the agencies consider are:

— Company earnings over a period of years to assess stability and sources of profits and control over expenses. The agencies look at product mix as well as the company's underwriting record and investment strategies.

— Capital adequacy and operating leverage. Capital is the cushion that allows a company to keep its commitments even if the value of its assets falls or its liabilities increase. In assessing capital adequacy, rating agencies look at the particular risks involved in each product line, and at the quality of the company's investments, and the ratio of its assets to its liabilities.

— Liquidity's importance when cash being paid out increases unexpectedly relative to cash coming in. Rating agencies consider the effect on a company's available cash under interest rate scenarios that would adversely affect the market value of its stock, bond and real estate holdings.

— Investment performance and investment risk management. A high concentration of particular types of assets may be cause for concern.

— The strength of the reinsurance program. Reinsurance provides companies a cushion against losses, particularly catastrophic losses. Following Hurricane Andrew, 10 insurance companies became insolvent. A major factor causing some of these companies to go out of business was a lack of adequate reinsurance.

— Management ability, experience and integrity.

The ratings express the agencies' opinions about an insurer's financial condition at a specific point in time. They can provide a useful snapshot for insurance buyers and reporters. But as history has shown, a high rating is no guarantee the company won't encounter severe financial problems. Insolvencies can occur because of an unprecedented external event — the 10 insurance companies may have failed as a result of Hurricane Andrew, for example — or the financial data they presented to raters may have been false or outdated.

Real estate investments: Life insurers typically own two types of real estate investment — commercial mortgage loans and real property. Insurers must report to regulators mortgages on which interest is more than 90 days overdue; mortgages in the process of foreclosure; and mortgages that are in foreclosure, whose underlying collateral becomes part of the insurer's real estate holdings. One measure of an insurer's financial health is the total amount of its problem mortgages as a percentage of its net worth.

Redlining: It's illegal for insurers to redline — i.e., *refuse to lend money or issue insurance based only on geographic area*. In general, an insurer must make any type of coverage it sells in any state available throughout the state, unless it can demonstrate that a specific area presents a much higher degree of risk — such as homeowners insurance in flood and windstorm-prone coastal areas. In such cases, coverage for above-average risks may be available from government-sponsored insurance pools.

All insurers licensed in a state are usually required to participate in that state's insurance pools for types of coverage that they sell. (See **Assigned risk plans; FAIR Plans; Beach and Windstorm Plans**)

Regulation: The insurance business is state-regulated. (See **Antitrust laws; McCarran-Ferguson**) State insurance laws are administered by insurance departments, whose job includes *approval of rates and policy forms, investigation of company practices, review of annual financial statements, periodic examination of books, and liquidation of insolvent insurers*.

The chief insurance regulator, called the insurance commissioner or superintendent, is elected or appointed by the governor, depending on the state, and is responsible for seeing that insurance companies remain solvent, that pricing is fair and reasonable, and that insurance stays available. Each state sets its own requirements for company reserves. (See **Solvency; Rate regulation**)

Reinsurance: Insurers buy insurance, too. It's called reinsurance. A reinsurer assumes part of a risk — and part of the premium — originally taken by the insurer, which is called the primary company. Reinsurance effectively increases an insurance company's capital and therefore its capacity to sell increased amounts of coverage. (See **Capacity**)

Reinsurers have their own reinsurers, called retrocessionaires. Reinsurance is a global business. Some of the world's biggest reinsurance companies are European and Asian firms. The billions of dollars worth of risk assumed by the American insurance industry are spread across an international network of reinsurance and retrocession.

As an international business with only corporate clients (who are presumed to be financially sophisticated), reinsurance is less regulated than primary insurance. However, U.S. reinsurers file their financial statements with state regulators and are subject to periodic examination, just as primary insurers are. And in assessing an insurance company's strength, regulators take into consideration the amount of reinsurance it carries, and whether or not its reinsurers are state-licensed.

The statutory accounting used by insurance regulators doesn't credit insurers' balance sheets for non-admitted reinsurance — i.e., reinsurance from an unlicensed company — as it does for admitted reinsurance. (See **Non-admitted insurer**)

Passing some or all of its risk to reinsurers doesn't relieve an insurance company of its obligation to pay claims. Reinsurers don't pay the insurance company's policyholder claims; rather, the reinsurer reimburses the insurance company for claims it has paid.

Reinsurance, life insurance policies: See **Assumption reinsurance**

Reinsurance policies: There are two basic kinds of reinsurance: *Treaty reinsurance* is a standing agreement between an insurer and reinsurer. The reinsurer automatically accepts specific percentages of entire classes of the insurer's business — 20 percent of its book of auto insurance, for example — up to pre-agreed limits.

Insurers seek *facultative reinsurance* for specific individual risks unusual or big enough so that they aren't covered in reinsurance treaties — an oil rig or jumbo jet, for example. The reinsurer isn't bound by contractual obligation to accept any facultative risk, but is free to assess each such risk on its own merits.

Renters insurance: Tenants or renters insurance is a form of homeowners policy. It covers the policyholder's belongings against perils including fire, theft, windstorm, hail, explosion, vandalism, accidental discharge of steam from heating systems, riot or civil commotion, even volcanic eruption. The policy also provides personal liability coverage for damage the policyholder and his or her dependents cause to third parties.

Renters policies also provide *additional living expenses* (also known as loss-of-use coverage) if the policyholder is forced to live elsewhere while his or her dwelling is being repaired.

Most renters policies also include some coverage for any improvements the tenant has made to the property, even though he or she doesn't own it.

Renters policy limits: The renter's possessions can be covered for their *replacement value*, which is the cost of replacing them with items of like kind and quality, or for their *actual cash value*. Actual cash value is replacement cost minus depreciation.

Replacement cost contents insurance: Insurance that pays the dollar amount needed to replace damaged personal property with items of like kind and quality, without deducting for depreciation.

Replacement cost dwelling insurance: Insurance that pays the policyholder the cost of replacing the damaged property without deduction for depreciation, but limited by the maximum dollar amount indicated on the declarations page of the policy.

Reserves: See **Loss reserves; Capital & surplus**

Residual market: See **Assigned risk plans; Beach and Windstorm Plans; FAIR Plans**

Retention: The amount of risk retained by an insurance company, i.e., not reinsured.

Retrocessionaires: See **Reinsurance**

Retrospective rating: A method of permitting the final premium for a risk to be adjusted, subject to an agreed-upon maximum and minimum limit, based on the actual loss experience. Retrospective rating is available to big commercial insurance buyers.

Rider: See **Endorsement**

Risk: This is a word with two meanings for insurers: 1. The chance of loss, i.e., a peril insured against; 2. The person or entity that is insured.

Risk-based capital: The National Association of Insurance Commissioners (NAIC) is working to develop formulas that would require insurers to be capitalized according to the riskiness of their investments and the type of insurance they sell. Higher-risk investment portfolios and/or higher risk types of insurance would necessitate higher levels of capital. The NAIC recommendations will be formalized as model insurance regulations. Each state legislature decides whether or not to adopt them.

Risk management: Management of the varied risks to which a business firm or association might be subject. It involves analyzing all exposures to gauge the likelihood of loss, and choosing among the options to minimize that loss. These options typically include reducing or eliminating the risk with safety measures, buying insurance, and self-insuring.

Risk retention groups: See **Self-insurance**

S

Salvage: 1) *Damaged property an insurer takes over, after it has paid a claim, to reduce its loss.* Insurers that paid claims on ships and cargoes lost at sea more than 100 years ago now have salvage rights to sunken treasure recovered from their wrecks, for example. 2) Salvage charges are the costs associated with recovering property exposed to a peril — saving the cargo of a foundering ship, for example.

Schedule: A list of individual items or groups of items that are covered under one policy.

SEC filings: Publicly-held insurance companies make periodic financial disclosures to the Securities and Exchange Commission (SEC) as well as to state insurance regulators. Among the major SEC filings are:

The **10-K**, an annual financial statement of the company's total sales, revenue, and pre-tax operating income. The 10-K also lists company sales by separate classes of products for each of its separate lines of business, for each of the past five years. A less comprehensive version of this information is contained in the company's **10-Q**, which is filed quarterly, and includes comparative data for the same period of the previous year.

Publicly-traded companies must also report to the SEC any material event that might affect the company or the value of its shares. The SEC defines "material" as any event an average prudent investor should know about before deciding whether to buy, sell, or hold shares. The required report, an **8-K**, must be filed with the SEC within one month of the occurrence of the material event.

Other SEC filings that are useful to investors and to reporters: *Form 3*, which lists the number of shares, warrants, rights, and convertible bonds owned by company insiders. Insiders include all holders of 10 percent or more of an SEC-registered company's stock, and all company directors and officers, whether or not they own any shares. *Form 4* reports any changes in the stock holdings of company insiders. It must be filed within 10 days of the end of the month in which there has been a major change in ownership. SEC filings are part of the public record.

Self-insurance: In the simplest sense, self-insurance means *assuming a financial risk oneself, instead of paying an insurance company to take it.* Every policyholder is a self-insurer to the extent of his or her deductible and coinsurance, and to the extent that his or her financial losses exceed policy limits.

However, the term "self-insurance" usually applies to group self-insurance, or the practice of employers (and, frequently, unions) to assume all or part of the responsibility for paying the health insurance claims of their employees or members.

Virtually all big corporations self-insure many of their risks and so do many smaller companies. Corporate self-insurance was initiated by Fortune 500 companies in the 1970s (partly for tax reasons that are no longer current) and partly to reduce insurance costs and escape the ups and downs of the property/casualty cycle (see **Property/casualty cycle**) in which periods of plentiful, cheap coverage are succeeded by periods of insurance scarcity and high premiums.

Many smaller companies followed suit in the mid-1980s, when liability insurance was very expensive and for some firms, unavailable. Self-insurance by small companies was facilitated by the federal Risk Retention Act of 1981 (broadened in 1986), which allowed groups of companies to band together as self-insurers. A risk retention group must be chartered and licensed as an insurer under the laws of at least one state.

The insurance industry calls mechanisms used to fund self-insurance "alternative markets." These mechanisms include captives — insurers that are wholly-owned by one or more non-insurers for the purpose of providing their owners with coverage — and risk retention groups formed by members of similar professions or businesses.

By the end of the 1980s, captives and other forms of self- insurance accounted for about one-third of U.S. insurance premiums. Providing administrative services to captives has become an important source of fee income for many insurance brokers and companies.

Self-insurance/legal issues: More than half of all employees now work for companies that self-insure their health benefits, using their own assets and employee contributions (in the form of deductibles and copayments) to pay claims. Under the Employee Retirement Income Security Act (ERISA) of 1974, self-insured firms are exempt from state insurance laws mandating the illnesses that group health insurers must cover. This means a self-insured employer may be able to reduce or eliminate coverage for extremely expensive, catastrophic illnesses — illnesses that by state law must be included in coverage sold by insurers.

The U.S. Supreme Court in 1992 refused to review the case of an employer who set a separate $5,000 limit on total lifetime health benefits for AIDS, while covering treatment of other illnesses for up to $1 million.

The employer, Texas-based H&H Music Co., changed from a group insurance policy to a self-insurance plan and imposed the limit for AIDS-related claims after one of its employees, John McGann, contracted AIDS. McGann sued H&H Music for discrimination and lost. A federal appeals court found H&H Music had acted within its rights as a self-insured firm.

Many lawyers believe the ERISA exemption has been rendered moot by the Americans with Disabilities Act (ADA), enacted in 1992, several years after the H&H Music case. ADA bars discrimination in employment and benefits against qualified job applicants and workers who are disabled. AIDS is a protected disability under the law.

The nation's commercial health insurers have strongly opposed all separate limits on benefits payable to people with AIDS, taking the position that it should be treated as any other physical disease for insurance purposes. (See **Accelerated death benefits; AIDS**)

Soft market: A market environment in which insurance is plentiful and sold at a lower cost; i.e., a buyer's market. (See **Property/casualty cycle**)

Solvency: One of insurance regulators' primary responsibilities is making sure insurance companies remain solvent, and thus have the ability to pay the claims of their policyholders. Solvency regulation varies from state to state, but typically includes:

1. Minimum capital and surplus requirements. These dollar amounts currently vary considerably from state to state, and don't take into account the quality of an insurer's assets or the kind of insurance products it sells. The National Association of Insurance Commissioners is developing model capital standards that address these issues. (See **Capital & surplus; Risk-based capital**)
2. Statutory accounting conventions, which impose more conservative financial standards than generally accepted accounting procedures. (See **Accounting**)

3. Rules that limit insurance company investments and/or corporate activities that are deemed risky to policyholders.
4. The application of financial ratio tests (See **Capital & surplus; Early warning system**)
5. Disclosure of financial data. Every insurer submits a comprehensive annual financial statement to regulators. Publicly-owned insurance companies must also comply with disclosure requirements of the Securities and Exchange Commission. (See **SEC filings**)

Spread of risk: An insurance company would rather sell hurricane insurance in six states than in one town for the same reason an investor puts money into many stocks rather than one: There's much less risk of taking a big hit. *Spread of risk minimizes the danger that all policyholders will have losses at the same time.* Some perils — floods, earthquakes and war among them — don't offer good spread of risk and as a result, aren't readily insurable. People don't tend to buy earthquake insurance unless they live in an area highly vulnerable to earthquakes. (See **Adverse selection**)

State funds: See **Guaranty associations**

Statistical data: The insurance business is based on the spread of risk. The more widely risk is spread, the more accurately loss can be estimated. An insurance company can more accurately estimate the probability of loss on 100,000 houses than on 10 houses. From its inception, the insurance industry has pooled statistical information.

Initially, property/casualty insurers shared their loss and expense data with rating services. These organizations or bureaus used the information to create standardized policies and develop rates which were adopted by a majority of insurers. Some bureaus required that members adhere to their rates.

Regulators viewed the early rating bureaus as a form of policyholder protection against insurance company insolvencies: Insurers that agreed to use rating bureau premiums wouldn't underprice their policies to gain market share and wind up going broke. In 1945, the McCarran-Ferguson Act *continued the limited exemption from federal antitrust law that allowed insurers to continue sharing data.*

Most of the rating bureaus were consolidated into the Insurance Services Office (ISO) in 1971. ISO never required adherence to its advisory rates, and most companies priced their products below the ISO rate. But because ISO rates were always high enough to ensure insurer solvency, they served as a benchmark for sound pricing for insurance regulators and for small insurers, whose own loss experience wasn't broad enough to be actuarially reliable. ISO stopped issuing advisory rates in 1989. It still issues estimates of future losses and loss adjustment expenses, such as claims handling and legal defense. (See **Antitrust laws**)

Statutory accounting: See **Accounting**

Stock insurance company: See **Insurance company**

Structured settlement: *An agreement to pay a designated person a specified sum of money in periodic payments, usually for his or her lifetime, instead of in a single lump sum payment.* Structured settlements typically are used to pay court-ordered or privately-agreed upon damages to injured claimants or their survivors. Structured settlements are also used to pay lottery winners. In both cases, the settlement is funded with an annuity. (See **Annuity**)

Subrogation: The legal process by which an insurance company, after paying a loss, seeks to recover the amount of the loss from another party who is legally liable for it. After the April 1992 flood in downtown Chicago, for example, several insurers brought action for subrogation against the city of Chicago and its contractor, which had caused the flood by accidentally piercing an underwater tunnel.

Superfund: The Comprehensive Environmental Response, Compensation and Liability Act, *a federal law enacted in 1980 to initiate cleanup of the nation's abandoned hazardous waste dump sites*, and to respond to accidents that release hazardous substances into the environment. This law, commonly known as Superfund, also enabled government agencies to recover monies from private parties identified as causing pollution and to compel responsible parties to clean up sites on their own. A tax was established on chemical feed stocks, crude oil and imported petroleum to provide initial funding for cleanup. However, the bulk of the funding was to come from liability actions against polluters.

The two other federal laws regulating environmental pollution that impact on insurance are the Resource Conservation and Recovery Act and the Motor Carrier Act. Polluters are liable for environmental damage and injuries caused by hazardous substances under common law and under the liability provisions set out in these federal acts.

The Superfund law applies the doctrine of joint and several liability, under which all parties that contributed to polluting a site, however minutely or unwittingly, are equally and fully liable for clean-up costs. The law also applies retroactively. Thus, even companies that followed the laws on waste disposal prior to 1980 are held liable. The insurance industry opposes these parts of the law, which it believes have made the law unworkable and resulted in vast expenditures of money on litigation which could better have been spent on cleanup. A 1992 Rand Corp. study of data from four insurers and five large industrial firms concluded that 88 percent of the monies spent on Superfund-related claims are spent in resolving disputes about who is responsible for cleanup.

The cost of cleaning up the nation's known hazardous waste sites, including nuclear weapons plants owned by the federal government, has been estimated at between $752 billion and $1 trillion. (See **Pollution insurance**)

Surety bond: Contractors usually are required to purchase surety bonds, if they are working on public projects. A surety bond guarantees to one party that another (the contractor) will perform specified acts, usually within a stated period of time. The surety company typically becomes responsible for fulfillment of a contract if the contractor defaults. In the case of a public works project, such as a road, that means that the surety bond protects taxpayers should a contractor go out of business.

Surplus lines: *Property/casualty coverage that isn't available from insurers licensed by the state — called admitted insurers — and must be purchased from a non-admitted carrier.* Surplus lines is coverage that often is sold by only a few carriers. An example is environmental liability insurance. (See **Non-admitted insurer**)

T

Term insurance: See **Life insurance**

Third party: In an insurance contract, a third party is anyone other than the policyholder and members of his or her family who are covered in the policy. The insured and the insurer are the first and second parties to the contract. Anyone else is a third party.

Title insurance: Insurance that indemnifies the owner of real estate in the event that his or her clear ownership of property is challenged by the discovery of faults in the title.

Tort: *A wrongful act, resulting in injury or damage, on which a civil action may be based.* This doesn't apply to breach of contract, for which action would be brought under contract law.

Tort law: The *body of law governing negligence, intentional interference, and other wrongful acts for which civil action can be brought,* except for breach of contract, which is covered by contract law.

During the 1980s, the rising cost of liability insurance, and the difficulty some buyers had obtaining it, stimulated interest in reforming the tort system. The insurance industry and the business community have pressed for reform in two major areas: changes in court procedures that would reduce the expense and delays in settling claims; and changes in tort law, including:

— the abolition or modification of joint and several liability, a rule under which defendants only minimally responsible for injury may be required to pay the full amount of the damages. (See **Pollution insurance**)

— modification of the collateral source rule of evidence, which bars the introduction of any information indicating that a person has been compensated or reimbursed by any source other than the defendant.

— limitation on punitive damages, which are intended to punish defendants who showed a wanton disregard for safety. Reform measures may limit the type of case in which such damages may be awarded, or require hearings to establish a case for punitive damages before they may be sought in court.

— caps on noneconomic damages, such as pain and suffering.

In the late 1980s, 45 states enacted tort reform legislation addressing at least one of these issues.

Treaty reinsurance: See **Reinsurance policies**

Twenty-four-hour coverage: Workers compensation coverage pays for work-related injuries and illness. Group health insurance benefits pay for non-occupational illnesses. An increasing number of employers and insurers believe that substantial cost savings are to be achieved by *eliminating the distinction between job-related and non-occupational illnesses and injuries, and integrating workers compensation and general health benefits* in 24-hour coverage.

But there are major legal obstacles to 24-hour coverage. Workers compensation is mandated by state law in 47 states, and it varies from one state to another. Group benefits are voluntary, and fall under federal laws like the Consolidated Omnibus Budget Reconciliation Act (COBRA) and the Employee Retirement Income Security Act (ERISA). Combining the two systems would require major structural changes among employers and insurers as well as legal changes, because the two coverages are separately administered.

Umbrella policy: *Coverage for losses above the limit of an underlying policy.* Umbrella coverage applies only to losses over a large dollar amount, but terms of coverage are sometimes broader than those of underlying policies.

Underinsurance: *The result of the policyholder's failure to buy sufficient insurance.* The coinsurance clause in many commercial insurance policies, for example, requires the policyholder to carry coverage equal to 100 percent of the cost of rebuilding, in order to receive full payment for each loss. A policyholder who doesn't meet this requirement is underinsured, and may only receive a portion of the cost of replacing or repairing damaged items covered in his or her policy.

Underwriting: The basic role of an insurance company — *examining, accepting, or rejecting insurance risks, and classifying the ones that are accepted, in order to charge the appropriate premiums for them.*

Underwriting income: Insurers make money by underwriting (i.e., selling insurance) and by investing premiums received. Underwriting income is *the insurer's profit on the insurance sale, after all expenses and losses have been paid.* When premiums aren't sufficient to cover claims and expenses, the result is an underwriting loss.

The property/casualty insurance industry has experienced frequent cycles of underwriting losses in the past 20 years, and some lines of coverage — auto insurance, for example — haven't shown an underwriting profit in years. Insurers' underwriting losses typically have been more than offset by their investment income, allowing them to continue insurance operations and earn a profit for shareholders. (See **Investment income)**

Unearned premium: Insurance premiums typically are payable in advance and have not been fully earned until the policy period expires. Six months after the purchase of a $1,200 annual policy, for example, the insurer's earned premium is $600. The remaining $600 of premium is designated as unearned. If the insurance company canceled the policy at the six-month point, it would return the $600 of unearned premium — less an amount for administrative expenses — to the policyholder.

Uninsurable risk: See **Insurable risk**

Universal life insurance: *A flexible premium policy that combines protection against premature death with a savings account that typically earns a money market rate of interest.* The premiums, death benefit and cash value can be changed during the life of the policy, within stated limits. While there is no fixed premium, the policy will lapse if there isn't enough money in the cash account to cover mortality costs and administrative charges. Policyholders receive an annual statement showing credits and deductions in the policy's cash value. (See **Life insurance products; Whole life insurance**)

Urban insurance: See **FAIR Plans; Assigned risk plans; Catastrophe/riot and civil commotion**

Utilization review: A *program* included in many health care benefit plans, *in which medical treatments or hospital stays ordered by the insured person's medical providers are reviewed by the benefits provider (typically the insured's employer) or a third-party acting on its behalf.* The review assesses whether treatment is medically appropriate and in accordance with generally accepted standards of medical practice. (See **Health insurance/ managed care**)

V

Valued policy: A policy under which an insurer agrees to pay a specified amount of money — not related in any way to the extent of the loss — to or on behalf of the insured upon occurrence of a defined loss. Life insurance policies, for example, are valued policies.

Vandalism: The malicious or ignorant, often random, destruction or spoilage of another person's property.

Variable life insurance: *A policy that combines protection against premature death with a savings account that can be invested in a variety of stock, bond and money market mutual funds, at the policyholder's direction.* (See **Life insurance products**) Most variable life policies guarantee that the death benefit will not fall below a specified minimum.

Void: A term to describe a policy contract that for some reason specified in the policy becomes free of all legal effect. If critical information the policyholder gave when applying for coverage was untrue, for example, the policy would be voided.

Volcano coverage: Most homeowners policies cover damage caused by the eruption of a volcano. (See **Catastrophe/volcanic eruptions**)

W

Waiver: The surrender of a right or privilege which is known to exist.

War risk: War risk insurance is available only as a *special coverage on cargo in overseas ships, against the risk of being confiscated by a government in wartime.* War risk is excluded from standard ocean marine insurance, but can be separately purchased. Typically, it excludes cargo awaiting shipment on a wharf, or on ships after 15 days of arrival at a port.

Standard property/casualty policies typically cover damages caused as a result of acts of terrorism, but exclude coverage for acts of war. Life insurance policies issued to soldiers in time of war typically exclude war risk; at the war's end, the exclusion clause is removed and cannot thereafter be reinserted. The exclusion clause cannot be added to a life insurance policy already in force.

Whole life insurance: *The oldest kind of cash value life insurance, which combines protection against premature death with a savings account.* In traditional whole life insurance, premiums are fixed, guaranteed, and based on conservative interest and mortality assumptions. The premiums remain level throughout the life of the policy. The cash value is invested in the life insurance company's general investment account, and grows tax-deferred. (See **Life insurance products**)

Workers compensation: Workers compensation insurance *pays for medical care and physical rehabilitation of injured workers and replaces their lost wages while they're unable to work.* It also provides death benefits for the dependents of employees killed in work-related accidents. The benefit levels are set by state law. Created in 1911, workers compensation is mandatory for nearly all employees in all states except New Jersey, South Carolina and Texas.

As the 1990s began, corporate insurance buyers, insurers and regulators agreed that manifold problems in the workers compensation system had reached crisis proportions:

Workers compensation rates are mandated by state regulators. In many states, rate increases haven't kept pace with spiraling costs. The coverage has sustained severe losses for more than a decade. Many insurers have stopped selling it. Employers have been forced to buy coverage in state-mandated residual markets — insurance pools which by law must sell coverage to any employer unable to obtain it in the voluntary market. (Typically, all insurers licensed to sell workers compensation coverage in a state must participate in that state's residual market, whose losses are subsidized by voluntary market customers.)

There is general agreement that the workers compensation system badly needs reform. One reason the system now functions so badly is that it was designed for a very different environment from the one in which it now operates:

1) The definition of work-related injury has expanded considerably since 1911. Workers compensation was created to compensate employees who had suffered injuries like the loss of a limb. It's now called on to pay for soft tissue injuries, asbestos claims, repetitive motion trauma, stress-induced mental illness — injuries whose very existence was unknown in 1911. Some of these occupational diseases have an extremely long latency period, unlike the traumatic injuries for which workers compensation was created. As a result, many people can be exposed to the hazard — asbestos, for example — before its inherent danger is recognized, and measures are taken to safeguard against it.

2) As the definition of work-related injury has expanded, so has litigation associated with workers compensation coverage. This

has increased the cost of coverage. Workers compensation started as no-fault insurance. Employers agreed to pay for work-related injuries, no matter whose negligence caused them, and employees gave up the right to sue. But while state laws typically mandate the amount of compensation that must be paid for an injury like a lost hand, compensable damages for more recently discovered occupational injuries must be estimated.

The extent of the partial permanent disability caused by a soft tissue injury, for example, is a matter of opinion — and frequently litigated.

3) Workers compensation provides unlimited medical benefits, with no employee deductibles or coinsurance. This feature of the system can lead to expensive, unnecessary medical procedures. As government and business have imposed cost controls in public and private benefit programs, the cost of medical care in workers compensation has skyrocketed. The medical component of the average workers compensation claim grew 14 percent a year between 1980 and 1990.

4) Workers compensation premiums haven't kept pace with costs. In many states, regulators reluctant to increase employers' cost of doing business have repeatedly denied requested workers compensation rate increases. The result has been a vicious cycle: Insurers abandon the market as unprofitable. More and more employers buy coverage in the residual market, which must accept them at state-mandated rates. Residual market losses soar. They're passed as surcharges to the firms that can still buy coverage in the voluntary market — a dwindling base, because employers seek to escape residual market surcharges by self-insuring.

Insurers and employers are trying to control workers compensation costs by using the managed care techniques that have become common in group health benefit programs. These include forming relationships with preferred medical care providers who specialize in industrial injuries, establishing treatment protocols for injuries, and doing thorough audits of bills. (See **Twenty-four-hour-coverage**)

Write: To insure, underwrite, or accept an application for insurance.

Sources of Additional Information

The following associations are good sources of information for the media.

PROPERTY/CASUALTY INSURANCE, COMPANY ASSOCIATIONS

Insurance Information Institute.
Tel. 1-800-331-9146.
Fax. 212-732-1916.

A primary source for information, analysis and referral on insurance subjects. 110 William Street, New York, NY 10038.

Washington, DC Media Office.
Tel. 202-833-1580.
Fax. 202-223-5779.
1750 K Street, NW, Suite 1101,
Washington, DC 20006.

I.I.I. Affiliated Offices

Texas Subscriber Office.
Tel. 512-476-7025.
Fax. 512-476-1378.
800 Brazos Street, Suite 4220, Austin, TX 78701.

Washington Insurance Council.
Tel. 206-624-3330.
Fax. 206-624-1975.
1904 Third Avenue, Suite 925, Seattle, WA 98101-1123.

Western Insurance Information Service/
Insurance Information Institute
Home Office.
Tel. 213-738-5333.
Fax. 213-738-7556.
3530 Wilshire Blvd., Suite 1610, Los Angeles, CA 90010.
Beaverton, Oregon Office.
Tel. 503-643-6355.
Fax. 503-641-3338.
11855 S.W. Ridgecrest Drive, Suite 107, Beaverton, OR 97005.
Englewood, Colorado Office.
Tel. 303-790-0216.
Fax. 303-790-0433.
6565 South Dayton St., Suite 2400, Englewood, CO 80111.
Northern California Office.
Tel. 510-277-8799.
Fax. 510-277-8798.
3000 Executive Parkway, Suite 300, San Ramon, CA 94583.

Insurance Information Institute Representatives
Central States Representative.
Tel. 913-768-4700.
Fax. 913-768-4900.
130 North Cherry Street, Suite 202, Olathe, KS 66061.
Southeastern States Representative.
Tel. 770-509-1725.
Fax. 770-509-7811.
1225 Johnson Ferry Road, Suite 220, Marietta, GA 30068.

Alliance of American Insurers.
Tel. 708-330-8500.
Fax. 708-330-8602.

A trade association of property and casualty insurers providing educational, legislative, promotional and safety services to its members. 1501 Woodfield Rd., Suite 400 West, Schaumburg, IL 60173-4980.

American Insurance Association.
Tel. 202-828-7100.
Fax. 202-293-1219.

A trade and service organization for property and casualty insurance companies; provides a forum for the discussion of problems; provides safety, promotional and legislative services. 1130 Connecticut Avenue, NW, Suite 1000, Washington, DC 20036.

American Insurance Services Group, Inc.
Tel. 212-669-0400.
Fax. 212-669-0535.

Wholly-owned subsidiary of the American Insurance Association, administers seven industry service organizations. They are the Index System, Property Insurance Loss Register, Premium Audit Advisory Service, Property Claim Services, Engineering & Safety Service, A-PLUS (Automated Property Loss Underwriting System) and Claims Settlement Service. 85 John Street, New York, NY 10038.

National Association of Independent Insurers.
Tel. 708-297-7800.
Fax. 708-297-5064.

Trade association of fire, casualty and surety insurers. 2600 River Road, Des Plaines, IL 60018.

National Association of Mutual Insurance Companies.
Tel. 317-875-5250.
Fax. 317-879-8408.

Trade association of property and casualty mutual insurance companies. 3601 Vincennes Road, Indianapolis, IN 46268-0700.

LIFE AND HEALTH INSURANCE, COMPANY ASSOCIATIONS

American Council of Life Insurance.
Tel. 202-624-2000.
Fax. 202-624-2319.

Trade association responsible for the public affairs, government, legislative and research aspects of the life insurance business. 1001 Pennsylvania Ave., NW, Suite 500 South, Washington, DC 20004-2599.

Health Insurance Association of America.
Tel. 202-824-1600.
Fax. 202-824-1722.

Central source of health insurance information. Trade association responsible for public relations, government relations, legislation and research on behalf of the private commercial health insurance industry. 555 13th Street, NW, Suite 600 East, Washington, DC 20004-1109.

ASSOCIATIONS AND GROUPS THAT CAN DISCUSS INSURANCE ISSUES FROM A BUYER'S PERSPECTIVE

Agents and brokers

American Association of Managing General Agents.
Tel. 816-444-3500.
Fax. 816-444-0330.

Association of managing general agents of insurers. 9140 Ward Parkway, Kansas City, MO 64114.

Council of Insurance Agents & Brokers.
Tel. 202-547-6616.
Fax. 202-546-0597.
Trade organization dedicated to safeguarding the public interest, preserving a competitive market, and working with others for the good of the insurance business and the public. 316 Pennsylvania Ave., SE, Suite 400, Washington DC 20003-1146.

Independent Insurance Agents of America, Inc.
Tel. 703-683-4422.
Fax. 703-683-7556.
Trade association of independent insurance agents. 127 S. Peyton Street, Alexandria, VA 23314.

National Association of Health Underwriters.
Tel. 202-223-5533.
Fax. 202-785-2274.
Professional association of persons who sell and service disability income and hospitalization and major medical health insurance. 1000 Connecticut Ave., NW, Suite 810, Washington, DC 20036.

National Association of Insurance Brokers, Inc.
Tel. 202-628-6700.
Fax. 202-628-6707.
Trade association of commercial insurance brokers. 1300 I Street, NW, Suite 900 East, Washington, DC 20005.

National Association of Life Underwriters.
Tel. 202-331-6000.
Fax. 202-835-9601.
Professional association representing life insurance agents. 1922 F Street, NW, Washington, DC 20006.

National Structured Settlements Trade Association.

Tel. 202-797-5108.

Fax. 202-332-2301.

Trade association representing consultants, insurers and others who are interested in the resolution and financing of tort claims through periodic payments. 1420 16th Street, NW, Washington, DC 20036.

Professional Insurance Agents.

Tel. 703-836-9340.

Fax. 703-836-1279.

Trade association of independent insurance agents. 400 N. Washington Street, Alexandria, VA 22314.

Consumer groups

American Association of Retired Persons.

Tel. 202-434-2277.

Organization devoted to improving every aspect of living for older people. 601 E Street, NW, Washington, DC 20049.

CFA Insurance Group.

Tel. 202-387-6121.

Established to advance the consumer interest on insurance issues through advocacy and education. 1424 16th Street, NW, Suite 604, Washington, DC 20036.

Consumer Federation of America.

Tel. 202-387-6121.

A nonprofit public interest organization. 1424 16th Street, NW, Suite 604, Washington, DC 20036.

Corporate insurance buyers

Risk and Insurance Management Society, Inc.

Tel. 212-286-9292.

Fax. 212-986-9716.

Organization of corporate buyers of insurance, which makes known to insurers the insurance needs of business and industry, supports loss prevention, and provides a forum for the discussion of common objectives and problems. 655 3rd Ave., New York, NY 10017.

Health maintenance organizations

Group Health Association of America.

Tel. 202-778-3200.

Fax. 202-331-7487.

National association of health maintenance organizations. 1129 20th Street, NW, Suite 600, Washington, DC 20036-3403.

INDEPENDENT ORGANIZATIONS THAT COVER THE INSURANCE INDUSTRY AND RELATED ISSUES

A M. Best Co.

Tel. 908-439-2200.

Fax. 908-439-2433.

A rating agency that reports on the financial condition of insurance companies. Ambest Road, Oldwick, NJ 08858.

Conning & Company

Tel. 203-527-1131.

Fax. 203-520-1504.

A company providing asset management, research and private equity services to the insurance industry. CityPlace II, 185 Asylum Street, Hartford, CT 06103-4105.

Duff & Phelps Credit Rating Company.

Tel. 312-368-3157.

Fax. 312-368-3155.

An organization that analyzes insurance company claims-paying ability. 55 East Monroe Street, Chicago, IL 60603.

Employee Benefits Research Institute.

Tel. 202-659-0670.

Fax. 202-775-6312.

An organization that contributes to the development of effective and responsible public policy in the field of employee benefits through research, publications, educational programs, seminars and direct communication. 2121 K Street, NW, Suite 600, Washington, DC 20037.

Moody's Investor's Service Inc.

Tel. 212-553-1658.

Fax. 212-553-4062.

A rating organization that analyzes an insurance company's ability to discharge senior policyholder debt obligations and claims. The ratings are based on an analysis of the insurance company and on its relationship to its parent, subsidiaries, and/or affiliates. 99 Church Street, New York, NY 10007.

Standard & Poor's Corporation.

Tel. 212-208-1527.

Fax. 212-412-0437.

An organization that rates companies according to their claims-paying ability. 25 Broadway, New York, NY 10004.

INDUSTRY ASSOCIATIONS THAT ARE SOURCES OF STATISTICAL INFORMATION

American Association of Insurance Services.
Tel. 708-595-3225.
Fax. 708-595-4647.
Rating, statistical and advisory organization, principally of small and medium-sized property/casualty companies. 1035 S. York Rd., Bensenville, IL 60106.

Insurance Research Council.
Tel. 708-871-0255.
Fax. 702-871-0260.
Provides the public and the insurance industry with timely research information relevant to public policy issues affecting risk and insurance. 211 South Wheaton Ave., Suite 410, Wheaton, IL 60187.

Insurance Services Office, Inc.
Tel. 212-898-6000.
Fax. 212-898-5525.
Provides research, advisory, rating, actuarial, statistical and other services relating to property and casualty insurance, including the development of policy forms, rates, premiums and related services for monoline and multiple line coverages. 7 World Trade Center, New York, NY 10048-1199.

Life Insurance Marketing and Research Association, Inc.
Tel. 203-688-3358.
Fax. 203-298-9555.
Principal source of life insurance industry sales and marketing statistics. Conducts research, provides management educational services, and prepares a wide range of publications for members all over the world. 300 Day Hill Rd., Windsor, CT 06095-4761.

Surety Association of America.

Tel. 908-494-7600.

Fax. 908-494-7609.

Statistical, rating, development and advisory organization for surety companies. 100 Wood Ave. South, Iselin, NJ 08830.

INSURANCE INDUSTRY ASSOCIATIONS THAT ARE USEFUL SOURCES OF INFORMATION ON SPECIFIC TOPICS

Arbitration

Arbitration Forums, Inc.

Tel. 813-931-4004.

Fax. 813-931-4618.

Nonprofit corporation that arbitrates and mediates disputes over insurance-related matters. P.O. Box 271500, Tampa, FL 33688-1500.

Arson

Insurance Committee for Arson Control.

Tel. 212-669-9245.

Fax. 212-791-1807.

All-industry coalition that acts as a catalyst for insurers' anti-arson efforts and a liaison with government agencies and other groups devoted to arson control. 110 William St., New York, NY 10038.

Auto accidents

Advocates for Highway & Auto Safety.

Tel. 202-408-1711.

Fax. 202-408-1699.

Alliance of consumer, safety and insurance organizations dedicated to highway and auto safety. 750 First Street, NE, Suite 901, Washington, DC 20002.

Highway Loss Data Institute.
Tel. 703-247-1600.
Fax. 703-247-1678.
Nonprofit organization to gather, process and provide the public with insurance data concerned with human and economic losses resulting from highway accidents. 1005 North Glebe Road, Suite 800, Arlington, VA 22201.

Insurance Institute for Highway Safety.
Tel. 703-247-1500.
Fax. 703-247-1678.
Traffic safety organization supported by automobile insurers. 1005 North Glebe Road, Suite 800, Arlington, VA 22201.

Catastrophes

Federal Emergency Management Agency.
Tel. 202-646-4600.
Fax. 202-646-4086.
The central agency within the Federal government for emergency planning, preparedness, mitigation, response and recovery. 500 C Street, SW, Washington, DC 20472.

Insurance Institute for Property Loss Reduction.
Tel. 617-722-0200.
Fax. 617-722-0202.
An insurance industry-sponsored nonprofit organization dedicated to reducing losses, deaths, injuries and property damage resulting from natural hazards. 73 Tremont Street, Suite 510, Boston, MA 02108-3910.

Natural Disaster Coalition.
Tel. 202-783-2785.
Fax. 202-783-0837.

An alliance of insurance groups, public safety officials and consumer organizations formed to promote Federal legislation to create a catastrophe reinsurance fund and encourage hazard mitigation. 1301 Pennsylvania Ave., NW, Suite 305, Washington, DC 20004.

Property Claim Services (PCS).
Tel. 908-388-5700.
Fax. 908-388-0171.

A division of the American Insurance Services Group, Inc., PCS tracks all disasters that cause more than $5 million in insured property damage on a state-by-state and nationwide basis. 700 New Brunswick Ave., Rahway, NJ 07065.

Claims adjusting

National Association of Independent Insurance Adjusters.
Tel. 312-853-0808.
Fax. 312-853-3225.

Association of claims adjusters and firms operating independently on a fee basis for all insurance companies. 300 W. Washington St., Suite 805, Chicago, IL 60606-2001.

Computerized claims processing and communications

ACORD.
Tel. 914-620-1700.
Fax. 914-620-0808.

Industry-sponsored institute serving to improve the computer processing of insurance transactions through the insurance agency system. One Blue Hill Plaza, 15th Floor, Pearl River, New York 10965-8529.

Insurance Value Added Network Services.
Tel. 203-531-5200.
Fax. 203-532-2199.
Industry-sponsored organization offering data communications network linking agencies, companies and providers of data to the insurance industry. 777 West Putnam Ave., Greenwich, CT 06830-5102.

Credit insurance

Foreign Credit Insurance Association.
Tel. 212-306-5000.
Fax. 212-513-4704.
Offers credit insurance facilities for U.S. exporters. 40 Rector Street, 11th floor, New York, NY 10006.

Crop insurance

American Association of Crop Insurers.
Tel. 202-789-4100.
Fax. 202-408-7763.
Trade association of insurance companies to promote crop insurance. 1 Massachusetts Ave., NW, Suite 800, Washington, DC 20001.

Crop Insurance Research Bureau.
Tel. 913-338-0470.
Fax. 913-661-1640.
Crop insurance trade organization. 9200 Indian Creek Parkway, Suite 220, Overland Park, KS 66210.

National Crop Insurance Services, Inc.
Tel. 913-685-2767.
Fax. 913-685-3080.
National trade association of insurance companies writing hail insurance, fire insurance, and insurance against other weather perils to growing crops, with rating and research services for crop-hail and rain insurers. 7201 West 129th Street, Suite 200, Overland Park, KS 66213.

Flood insurance

Federal Insurance Administration.

Tel. 202-646-4600.

Fax. 202-646-3445.

Administers the federal flood insurance and crime insurance programs. 500 C Street, SW, Washington, DC 20472.

Fraud

See **American Insurance Services Group, Inc.** on page 115.

Coalition Against Insurance Fraud.

Tel. 202-393-7330.

Fax. 202-393-7329.

A coalition of insurance companies, government agencies and consumer groups that advocates Federal and state anti-fraud legislation and regulation and informs the public about the high cost of fraud. 1511 K Street, NW, Suite 622, Washington, DC 20005.

Insurance Cost Containment Service.

Tel. 312-368-0700.

Fax. 312-368-8336.

Assists insurance companies with property claims adjustment and arson and fraud claims investigation. 230 West Monroe St., Suite 310, Chicago, IL 60606.

International Association of Special Investigation Units.

Tel. 212-669-9274.

Fax. 212-791-1807.

Association of more than 870 insurance company SIU professionals representing the largest property and casualty insurance companies in the country. Organization acts as an education and communications resource in the industry's fight against fraud. c/o I.I.I., 110 William Street, New York, NY 10038.

MIB, Inc. (Medical Information Bureau).
Tel. 617-426-3660.
Fax. 617-329-3379.

A nonprofit membership organization of about 750 life insurance companies, which operates a confidential interchange of underwriting information on behalf of its members as an alert against fraud. This interchange enables MIB members to protect the interests of insurance consumers as well as the interests of life, health and disability insurers. 160 University Ave., Westwood, MA 02090.

National Insurance Crime Bureau.
Tel. 708-430-2430.
Fax. 708-430-2446.

Not-for-profit organization dedicated to fighting crime and vehicle theft. 10330 S. Roberts Rd., 3A, Palos Hills, IL 60465.

Insurance company insolvencies

National Conference of Insurance Guaranty Funds.
Tel. 317-464-8199.
Fax. 317-464-8180.

Advisory organization to the state guaranty fund boards; gathers and disseminates information regarding insurer insolvencies. Market Tower, Ten W. Market Street, Suite 1190, Indianapolis, IN 46204.

National Organization of Life and Health Insurance Guaranty Associations.
Tel. 703-481-5206.
Fax. 703-481-5209.

Nonprofit organization that assists its member companies in handling multistate insolvencies, acts as a clearing house for information, and provides a forum for resolution of issues and problems arising from the operation of the state life and health insurance guaranty associations. 13873 Park Center Road, Suite 329, Herndon, VA 22071.

International insurance

International Insurance Council.

Tel. 202-682-2345.

Fax. 202-682-4187.

Speaks for and coordinates the international noncommercial activitie of U.S. insurance and reinsurance companies. 1212 New York Ave., NW, Suite 250, Washington, DC 20005.

International Insurance Society, Inc.

Tel. 212-815-9290.

Fax. 212-815-9297.

A nonprofit membership organization whose mission is to facilitate international understanding, the transfer of ideas and innovations and the development of personal networks across insurance markets through a joint effort of leading executives and academics throughou the world. 101 Murray St., New York, NY 10007-2165.

Overseas Private Investment Corporation.

Tel. 202-336-8400.

Fax. 202-336-8799.

Self-sustaining U.S. government agency providing political risk insur-ance and finance services for U.S. investment in developing countries 1100 New York Ave., NW, Washington, DC 20527.

Legislation

Conference of Insurance Legislators.

Tel. 518-449-3210.

Fax. 518-432-5651.

Organization of chairmen of state legislative committees concerned with insurance-related matters. 122 South Swan Street, Albany, NY 12210.

Litigation

Defense Research Institute, Inc.

Tel. 312-944-0575.

Fax. 312-944-2003.

Service organization to improve the administration of justice and defense lawyers' skills. 750 North Lake Shore Drive, Suite 500, Chicago, IL 60611.

Institute For Civil Justice.

Tel. 310-393-0411.

Fax. 310-393-4818.

Organization formed within The Rand Corporation to perform independent, objective research and analysis concerning the civil justice system. 1700 Main St., P.O. Box 2138, Santa Monica, CA 90407-2138.

Marine insurance

American Institute of Marine Underwriters.

Tel. 212-233-0550.

Fax. 212-227-5102.

Promotes the interests of marine underwriters. 14 Wall Street, 8th Floor, New York, NY 10005.

Inland Marine Underwriters Association.

Tel. 212-233-7958.

Fax. 212-732-3451.

Forum for discussion of problems of common concern to inland marine insurers. 111 Broadway, 15th Floor, New York, NY 10006.

Nuclear insurance

American Nuclear Insurers.

Tel. 203-561-3433.

Fax. 203-561-4655.

Nonprofit association through which property and liability insurance is provided against hazards arising out of nuclear reactor installations and their operations. Town Center, Suite 300 S., 29 South Main Street, West Hartford, CT 06107-2430.

Prepaid legal services

American Prepaid Legal Services Institute.

Tel. 312-988-5751.

Fax. 312-988-5032.

National membership organization to provide information and technical assistance to lawyers, insurance companies, marketers and consumers, regarding group and prepaid legal services. 541 N. Fairbanks Ct., Chicago, IL 60611-3314.

Reinsurance

Reinsurance Association of America.

Tel. 202-638-3690.

Fax. 202-638-0936.

Trade association of property and casualty reinsurance companies, providing legislative services to members. 1301 Pennsylvania Ave., NW, Suite 900, Washington, DC 20004.

Residual insurance markets

Automobile Insurance Plans Service Office.

Tel. 401-946-2310.

Fax. 401-528-1350.

Develops and files rates and provides other services for state-mandated automobile insurance plans. 302 Central Ave., Johnston, RI 02919-5095.

Property Insurance Plans Service Office.
Tel. 617-371-4175.
Fax. 617-371-4177.
Provides technical assistance and administrative services to state property insurance plans. 27 School Street, Suite 302, Boston, MA 02108-3910.

Safety

National Safety Council.
Tel. 708-285-1121.
Fax. 708-285-1315.
Provides national support and leadership in the field of safety; publishes safety materials of all kinds. 1121 Spring Lake Drive, Itasca, IL 60143-3201.

State insurance regulators

National Association of Insurance Commissioners.
Tel. 816-842-3600.
Fax. 816-471-7004.
Organization of state insurance commissioners to promote uniformity in state supervision of insurance matters and to recommend legislation in the various state legislatures. 120 W. 12th Street, Suite 1100, Kansas City, MO 64105. See page 133 for a list of state insurance departments.

Title insurance

American Land Title Association.
Tel. 202-296-3671.
Fax. 202-223-5843.
Trade organization for title insurers, abstractors and agents. Performs statistical research and lobbying services. 1828 L Street, NW, Suite 705, Washington, DC 20036.

Workers Compensation

National Council on Compensation Insurance.

Tel. 407-997-1000.

Fax. 407-997-4774.

Develops and administers rating plans and systems for workers compensation insurance. 750 Park of Commerce Drive, Boca Raton, FL 33487.

Workers Compensation Research Institute.

Tel. 617-494-1240.

Fax. 617-494-5240.

Organization supported by insurers and employers, conducting research on public policy issues in the workers compensation system. 101 Main Street, Cambridge, MA 02142.

STATE INSURANCE DEPARTMENTS

The majority of state commissioners are appointed by state governors and serve at their pleasure. The states designated with an asterisk(*) presently elect insurance commissioners to four-year terms.

Alabama Department of Insurance.
Tel. 334-269-3550.
Fax. 334-240-3194.
135 South Union St., Room 200, Montgomery, AL 36130.

Alaska Department of Insurance.
Tel. 907-465-2515.
Fax. 907-465-3422.
P.O. Box 110805, Juneau, AK 99801.

American Samoa Office of the Governor.
Tel. 011-684-633-4116.
Fax. 011-684-633-2269.
Pago Pago, AS 96799.

Arizona Department of Insurance.
Tel. 602-912-8400.
Fax. 602-912-8452.
2910 North 44th Street, Suite 210, Phoenix, AZ 85018-7256.

Arkansas Department of Insurance.
Tel. 501-686-2900.
Fax. 501-686-2913.
1123 South University Ave., Suite 400, University Tower Bldg., Little Rock, AR 72204-1699.

California Department of Insurance.*
Tel. 916-445-5544.
Fax. 916-445-5280.
300 Capitol Mall, Suite 1500, Sacramento, CA 95814.

Colorado Department of Insurance.
Tel. 303-894-7499.
Fax. 303-894-7455.
1560 Broadway, Suite 850, Denver, CO 80202.

Connecticut Department of Insurance.
Tel. 203-297-3802.
Fax. 203-566-7410.
P.O. Box 816, Hartford, CT 06142-0816.

Delaware Department of Insurance.*
Tel. 302-739-4251.
Fax. 302-739-5280.
The Rodney Bldg., 841 Silver Lake Blvd., Dover, DE 19904.

District of Columbia Department of Insurance.
Tel. 202-727-8000 x3007.
Fax. 202-727-8055.
441 Fourth Street, NW, 8th Floor North, Washington, DC 20001.

Florida Department of Insurance.*
Tel. 904-922-3101.
Fax. 904-488-3334.
State Capitol, Plaza Level 11, Tallahassee, FL 32399-0300.

Georgia Department of Insurance.*
Tel. 404-656-2056.
Fax. 404-657-7493.
2 Martin L. King, Jr. Dr., Floyd Memorial Bldg., 704 West Tower, Atlanta, GA 30334.

Guam Department of Insurance.
Tel. 011-671-477-5106.
Fax. 011-671-472-2643.
378 Chalan San Antonio, Tamuning, GU 96911.

Hawaii Department of Insurance.
Tel. 808-586-2790.
Fax. 808-586-2806.
230 S. King St., 5th Floor, Honolulu, HI 96813.

Idaho Department of Insurance.
Tel. 208-334-4250.
Fax. 208-334-4398.
700 West State Street, 3rd Floor, Boise, ID 83720.

Illinois Department of Insurance.
Tel. 217-782-4515.
Fax. 217-782-5020.
320 W. Washington St., 4th Floor, Springfield, IL 62767.

Indiana Department of Insurance.
Tel. 317-232-2385.
Fax. 317-232-5251.
311 West Washington St., Suite 300, Indianapolis, IN 46204-2787.

Iowa Department of Insurance.
Tel. 515-281-5705.
Fax. 515-281-3059.
Lucas State Office Building, 6th Floor, Des Moines, IA 50319.

Kansas Department of Insurance.*
Tel. 913-296-7801.
Fax. 913-296-2283.
420 South West Ninth St., Topeka, KS 66612-1678.

Kentucky Department of Insurance.
Tel. 502-564-6027.
Fax. 502-564-6090.
215 West Main St., Frankfort, KY 40602.

Louisiana Department of Insurance.*
Tel. 504-342-5423.
Fax. 504-342-8622.
P.O. Box 94214, Baton Rouge, LA 70801-9214.

Maine Department of Insurance.
Tel. 207-624-8475.
Fax. 207-582-8716.
State Office Building, State House, Station 34, Augusta, ME 04333.

Maryland Department of Insurance.
Tel. 410-333-2521.
Fax. 410-333-6650.
501 St. Paul Pl., Stanbalt Building, 7th Floor-South, Baltimore, MD 21202-2272.

Massachusetts Department of Insurance.
Tel. 617-727-7189.
Fax. 617-727-7189 x299.
280 Friend St.. Boston, MA 02114.

Michigan Department of Insurance.
Tel. 517-373-9273.
Fax. 517-335-4978.
611 West Ottawa St., 2nd Floor North, Lansing, MI 48933.

Minnesota Department of Insurance.
Tel. 612-296-6848.
Fax. 612-296-4328.
133 E. 7th Street, St. Paul, MN 55101.

Mississippi Department of Insurance.*
Tel. 601-359-3569.
Fax. 601-359-2474.
1804 Walter Sillers Building, Jackson, MS 39205.

Missouri Department of Insurance.
Tel. 314-751-4126.
Fax. 314-751-1165.
301 W. High St. 6 North, Jefferson City, MO 65102-0690.

Montana Department of Insurance.*
Tel. 406-444-2040.
Fax. 406-444-3497.
126 North Sanders, Mitchell Building, Room 270, Helena, MT 59601.

Nebraska Department of Insurance.
Tel. 402-471-2201.
Fax. 402-471-4610.
Terminal Bldg., 941 O St., Suite 400, Lincoln, NE 68508.

Nevada Department of Insurance.
Tel. 702-687-4270.
Fax. 702-687-3937.
1665 Hot Springs Rd., Suite 152, Carson City, NV 89710.

New Hampshire Department of Insurance.
Tel. 603-271-2261.
Fax. 603-271-1406.
169 Manchester St., Concord, NH 03301.

New Jersey Department of Insurance.
Tel. 609-292-5363.
Fax. 609-984-5273.
20 West State St., CN325, Trenton, NJ 08625.

New Mexico Department of Insurance.
Tel. 505-827-4601.
Fax. 505-827-4734.
P.O. Drawer 1269, Santa Fe, NM 87504-1269.

New York Department of Insurance.
Tel. 212-602-0429.
Fax. 212-602-0437.
160 W. Broadway, New York, NY 10013.

North Carolina Department of Insurance.*
Tel. 919-733-7349.
Fax. 919-733-6495.
Dobbs Building, 430 North Salisbury Street, Suite 4140, Raleigh, NC 27603.

North Dakota Department of Insurance.*
Tel. 701-328-2440.
Fax. 701-328-4880.
State Capitol Bldg., 5th Fl., 600 East Blvd., Bismarck, ND 58505-0320.

Ohio Department of Insurance.
Tel. 614-644-2658.
Fax. 614-644-3743.
2100 Stella Court, Columbus, OH 43215.

Oklahoma Department of Insurance.*
Tel. 405-521-2686.
Fax. 405-521-6635.
1901 North Walnut, Oklahoma City, OK 73105.

Oregon Department of Insurance.
Tel. 503-378-4271.
Fax. 503-378-4351.
350 Winter Street, NE, Room 200, Salem, OR 97310-0700.

Pennsylvania Department of Insurance.
Tel. 717-783-0442.
Fax. 717-772-1969.
1326 Strawberry Square, 13th Floor, Harrisburg, PA 17120.

Puerto Rico Department of Insurance.

Tel. 809-722-8686.

Fax. 809-722-4400.

Fernandez Juncos Station, 1607 Ponce de Leon Ave., Santurce, PR 00910.

Rhode Island Department of Insurance.

Tel. 401-277-2223.

Fax. 401-751-4887.

233 Richmond St., Suite 233, Providence, RI 02903-4233.

South Carolina Department of Insurance.

Tel. 803-737-6160.

Fax. 803-737-6229.

1612 Marion St., Columbia, SC 29202.

South Dakota Department of Insurance.

Tel. 605-773-3563.

Fax. 605-773-5369.

500 East Capitol, Pierre, SD 57501-3940.

Tennessee Department of Insurance.

Tel. 615-741-2241.

Fax. 615-741-4000.

Volunteer Plaza, 500 James Robertson Pkwy., Nashville, TN 37243-0565.

Texas Department of Insurance.

Tel. 512-463-6464.

Fax. 512-475-2005.

P.O. Box 149104, Austin, TX 78714-9104.

Utah Department of Insurance.
Tel. 801-538-3800.
Fax. 801-538-3829.
3110 State Office Bldg., Salt Lake City, UT 84114-1201.

Vermont Department of Insurance.
Tel. 802-828-3301.
Fax. 802-828-3306.
89 Main St. Drawer 20, Montpelier, VT 05620-3101.

Virgin Islands Department of Insurance.
Tel. 809-774-2991.
Fax. 809-774-6953.
Kongens Gade #18, St. Thomas, VI 00802.

Virginia Department of Insurance.
Tel. 804-371-9694.
Fax. 804-371-9873.
1300 East Main St., Tyler Bldg., Richmond, VA 23219.

Washington Department of Insurance.*
Tel. 360-753-7301.
Fax. 360-586-3535.
Insurance Building, 14th Ave. & Water Street, P.O. Box 40255, Olympia, WA 98504-0255.

West Virginia Department of Insurance.
Tel. 304-558-3354.
Fax. 304-558-0412.
P.O. Box 50540, Charleston, WV 25305-0540.

Wisconsin Department of Insurance.

Tel. 608-266-0102.

Fax. 608-266-9935.

121 E. Wilson St., Madison, WI 53702.

Wyoming Department of Insurance.

Tel. 307-777-7401.

Fax. 307-777-5895.

Herschler Building, 122 W. 25th St.-3rd Floor East, Cheyenne, WY 82002-0440.

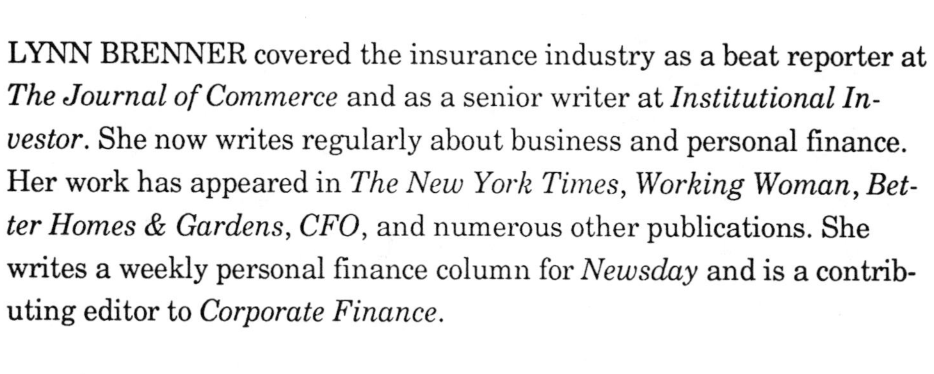

LYNN BRENNER covered the insurance industry as a beat reporter at *The Journal of Commerce* and as a senior writer at *Institutional Investor*. She now writes regularly about business and personal finance. Her work has appeared in *The New York Times*, *Working Woman*, *Better Homes & Gardens*, *CFO*, and numerous other publications. She writes a weekly personal finance column for *Newsday* and is a contributing editor to *Corporate Finance*.